GREEK ARCHITECTURE

Current and forthcoming titles in the Classical World Series

Classical World Series

GREEK ARCHITECTURE

R.A. Tomlinson

Bristol Classical Press

General Editor: John H. Betts
Series Editor: Michael Gunningham

This impression 2009
First published in 1989 by
Bristol Classical Press
an imprint of
Gerald Duckworth & Co. Ltd.
90-93 Cowcross Street, London EC1M 6BF
Tel: 020 7490 7300
Fax: 020 7490 0080
inquiries@duckworth-publishers.co.uk
www.ducknet.co.uk

A catalogue record for this book is available
from the British Library

ISBN 978 1 85399 115 8

Cover illustration:
The order of the Temple of Artemis, Magnesia
[drawing by Henry Buglass]

Contents

List of Illustrations

All line drawings have been made by Henry Buglass. The Photographs are my own, except for some nineteenth-century photographs of Classical architecture in Athens, which are from the collection made by Sir Lawrence Alma-Tadema, and now in the library of the University of Birmingham. Most of these are by the distinguished American photographer William J. Stillman (for an assessment of Stillman's achievement as a photographer, see *Poetic Localities*, ed. Anne Ehrenkranz et al., New York, 1988).

Fig. 1. The east end of the Parthenon (Stillman, 1869). Very little repair has been carried out, and the lower part of the apse inserted when the Parthenon was converted into a church can be seen behind the four central columns of the façade. This apse closed the temple at what was originally its principle entrance: for the church, the entrance was now at the west end, and the internal dividing wall was removed. The remains of the apse were removed shortly after this photograph was taken.

Chapter 1
Introduction

What is architecture?

Architecture is the art of buildings. It is concerned with the way in which they are designed, the methods by which they are constructed. It depends, says Vitruvius (who wrote in the time of Augustus the most important treatise on architecture to survive from the Classical world), on order, arrangement, proportion, symmetry, propriety and economy. Buildings need to be constructed in the proper manner, in the light of their function, the traditions of the society which uses them and the resources which can be devoted to them. To understand ancient Greek buildings it is necessary to know how they respond to the needs of Greek society. They cannot be treated simply as works of art, or ancient monuments surviving in isolation – impressive and beautiful though the most important of them are.

Inevitably, there is a distinction between utilitarian structures such as the houses in which ordinary people lived and the more splendid and expensive buildings which were erected for religious or public purposes. The utilitarian structures are rarely designed as individual buildings, but rather conform to an established pattern (such structures are often described as examples of vernacular architecture). They are built of the cheapest material, which in Classical Greece usually means bricks made of unbaked mud. Their form may depend on the nature of the material, and the availability of timber – the most expensive item in their construction (when the Athenians, in the final stages of the Peloponnesian War, were under siege as a result of the military base established by the Spartans at Decelea, their Boeotian enemies removed, as desirable plunder, the timbers from the houses in the rural villages). Vernacular buildings are not the work of architects, and in this sense are not part of the art of architecture, though the traditions they conform to may well influence the more important architectural achievements of their period.

1

Architecture as an art

Architecture as an art means the major public buildings, which include an element of display and show, buildings which are there to impress as well as to be used. They are made, generally of superior materials, which in Classical Greece are shaped blocks of stone, ideally white marble. They are fitted together more carefully than is the case with the vernacular. They are more carefully proportioned, width to length to height, and the different elements in their elevation more carefully related to each other. In the most important of them, the size increases substantially beyond that of the vernacular houses, so that they stand out and dominate their surroundings. They may receive more elaborate decoration, and parts of them are carved and painted. All this makes them more expensive, in terms of materials and the amount of labour required in their construction. Only rarely in Greek cities can such buildings be put up at the expense of a private person and, if they are, the fact that he possesses the requisite wealth marks him out as an important individual in society. More often they are the achievement of the community, from the resources which belong to the city and its gods. For such buildings the city takes a lively interest in the whole process of construction, supervising the designer and the providers of building material, judging its quality and satisfying itself that everything is in accordance with the required standards.

The survival rate of Greek architecture

Such buildings are more durable than the mudbrick houses of ordinary people. They are built to last, and in the more important of them measures are taken which are intended as far as possible to avert the consequences of the earthquakes to which much of Greece is prone – though it is only in places which are free from the major dangers of earthquake, such as Athens, that Classical buildings have a chance of surviving intact, or reasonably intact. Earthquakes are the major destructive factor; but equally devastating, over the passage of time, is neglect. Where a building continues to be used as a building, its chances of survival are relatively high; but it may have to suffer modification if the form of use changes.

If it had not been for the mortar bomb lobbed into the Parthenon in the Venetian siege of 1687, that temple would still survive as a building rather than a ruin. But it had undergone important modifications since it ceased to be a temple, particularly when it was converted into a church (see fig. 1, p. viii). This had necessitated the demolition of the great east door in order to construct the apsidal end required in a church, and the removal of the interior cross wall to create a larger room. (For the Parthenon, as a temple, was not designed to admit the large congregations of worshippers who attend a Christian service.) Even so, most of the structure, the marble walls and marble colonnades remained unaltered, and externally there was little, if any, change to these parts. There was, however, another major change, and this occurred in what was the weak point of all Classical buildings. The roof was originally covered in durable but heavy marble tiles; but these were supported by wooden rafters and beams, and the woodwork inevitably decayed. So the roof had to be renewed entirely. This seems to have been done when the temple was turned into a church, and it differed in form from the original. The outer surrounding colonnade, included under the original roof, had no function for the church (indeed, it still retained most of its overtly pagan sculptural decoration). The new roof, therefore, was narrower, covering only the walled cella, or room, of the temple, which was used as the church. It was this roof which was blown off in the explosion. Roofs are crucially important. With a roof over it, a building remains a building and can be used. Remove it, and it becomes a ruin, subject to decay, and likely to be demolished for its materials. Without roofs, buildings of unbaked brick are simply washed away.

Thus the survival rate of Classical Greek architecture is not good. Very few examples still function as buildings: there is a small tomb-temple on the island of Thera which survives intact and as it was built, converted into a church, but this has a roof made out of massive pieces of stone, without any timber supports. On a more substantial scale, the great temple dedicated to Athena at Syracuse (probably as a thankoffering for the defeat of the Carthaginian attack in 480) still functions as a cathedral; but here there have been massive alterations: probably the temple passed through a roofless and derelict ruined stage before it was converted. An excellent example of the rule that abandoned buildings become ruins is the Ionic temple of Artemis Agrotera just outside the walls of Athens. This was converted (with substantial alteration) into a church, and was still an intact building, functioning as a church when the British architects Stuart and Revett visited Athens to study and measure the surviving ancient buildings in 1751. Shortly after this it was desecrated and therefore abandoned; it was demolished for building material, and when the site of it was excavated in the 1960s, only the slightest traces of its foundations were found.

'The study of ruins'

The study of Greek architecture is therefore essentially the study of ruins, as an examination of the photographs in this book will demonstrate. Only rarely is a ruin sufficiently well preserved to give an immediate impression of the original appearance, and even with the best preserved some mental adjustment is necessary. Thus superficially the temple of Hephaistos (the 'Theseum') overlooking the agora at Athens appears to be a complete temple; but it has lost its original roof (it was converted into a church, and given a mortared vaulted roof over the cella only). From certain angles – particularly from below, or close to – this is concealed, but the temple nevertheless lacks the decoration which once marked the lowest point of the original roof. The absence of a roof over the surrounding colonnade admits light in a way which would not have been possible in the original, and this destroys the pattern of light and shade created by the original architectural form which is as much part of the architecture as the stones of wall and columns.

The temple also lacks much of its applied decoration: the painted work now entirely faded, and the sculpture which filled the pediments (the gable ends) or stood above them. Paintwork invariably fades. Traces of paintwork survived in the Parthenon; recent atmospheric pollution has led to further deterioration, but they

Fig. 2. Temple of Hephaistos. Photograph, late 1870s, with Acropolis in background.

were more visible in the nineteenth century, when they were copied and studied by F.C. Penrose. The nature of colour work in Greek buildings was a subject of lively dispute in the nineteenth century. There are still many uncertainties, though the excavation of fourth- and third-century built tombs in Macedonia (which were decorated with temple-like facades and then deliberately concealed by being covered with earth) has produced several examples of Classical architectural paintwork in pristine state. These give us a much better idea of the original appearance of buildings.

Most Greek buildings are more thoroughly ruined than the temple of Hephaistos and the Parthenon; and visualizing their original appearance requires greater skill in supplying the elements which no longer survive *in situ*. Thus it is essential in the study of Greek buildings to be able to convert plans into the complete, three-dimensional elevation. In effect, this means repeating the work of the original architect who had to know what his building would look like from the moment he laid out the foundations. It is unlikely that ancient Greek architects made detailed scale plans on papyrus of the buildings they were commissioned to construct. Papyrus was an expensive material, and architects did not have either the accurate rulers or the arithmetical ability to prepare scale drawings. So the

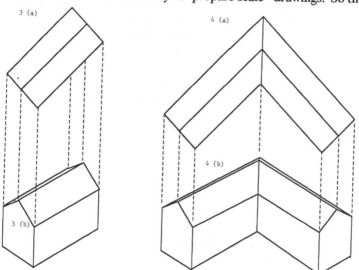

Fig. 3. Simple rectangular plan, and isometric projection of it.
Fig. 4. Two winged plan, and isometric projection of it.

essential arrangements of buildings had to conform to established and well-understood patterns. This kept them simple, and so most Greek buildings are straightforward rectangular boxes, with ridged roofs and gable ends. If the plan of a building is a simple rectangle, the general appearance of it can be visualised immediately. Figure 3a becomes figure 3b. Some buildings, it is true, have more complicated plans, but these are generally made up from series of rectangular boxes arranged in contact with each other. A simple example might be two extended stoas or porticoes, placed on the boundary of an open space – a sanctuary, or an agora. Thus figure 4a becomes figure 4b. Even the most complex public buildings, the exceptional Erechtheion on the Athenian Acropolis, or the Propylaia entrance to that sanctuary, merely extend the principle of rectangular elements placed in contact with each other. Only rarely is the box made circular rather than rectangular in plan: a mere handful of such buildings are known from the Classical Greek world.

Foundations, colonnades, columns

So when ancient Greek buildings are reduced, as so many of them are, to foundations, or even merely to the trenches cut into the native rock in which the foundations were placed, it is still possible to form some impression of the original standing building. To do this more accurately, more information is needed. What form did the elevation take? Did the exterior of the building consist of walls, or was it surrounded by a colonnade? If the foundations suggest two boxes, one inside the other, then there is a strong probability that the outer foundation supported a colonnade, the inner foundation a wall. In Greek buildings, colonnades are usually supported by continuous foundations in order to give added security, though rows of columns inside buildings, placed to support the roof and thus give a wider inner space, may have individual foundations. The foundations of the temple of Hephaistos may be drawn out schematically in this way (fig. 5). Since the building is relatively well preserved, we know which foundations supported walls and which supported columns, and so we can draw out most of the plan. The innermost foundations at present support nothing, but comparing them with other temples (such as that of Aphaia on the island of Aigina) we can be certain that they were for internal colonnades. Such colonnades were not inevitable (and, as we shall see, at Hephaistos they were an afterthought): where there are no foundations, no internal colonnades

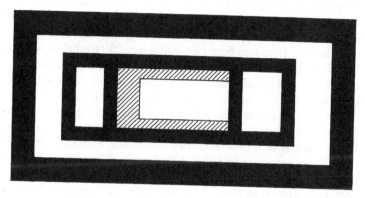

Fig. 5. Plan of foundations, temple of Hephaistos.

were constructed.

More accurate understanding of the original appearance of the building depends on the survival of elements from the superstructure. The less splendid buildings, such as stoas, might have colonnades which rested only on a single step, the position of which is easily determined by the foundations. Temples, however, usually rested on bases with a number of steps up to the colonnade. It is thus useful to be able to determine the position of the top step, since this gives us the line of the colonnade. If some of the steps are still *in situ*, this can be done easily. But even if they are dislodged, so long as there are blocks surviving from the different steps, the original position of the top step can be calculated: the lower blocks usually have marks on their upper surfaces which show where the next high step was placed. If we are fortunate, the top step (stylobate) will itself bear marks which show where the columns were placed, and from these – even if only a few survive – we can work out the original number of columns and their spacing. Even if there are no marks (or no surviving stylobate blocks), the spacing of the columns can be worked out from the blocks of the superstructure (entablature) they carried, for these were placed in accordance with the centre lines of the columns.

Still more information is required. Greek architecture employed two main types of column: one being traditional to the Greek mainland and called Doric (since it seems to have originated in Dorian Corinth, a confusing name as it is also used by non-Dorian cities of the mainland, such as Athens), the other originating in the islands of the Aegean or in the East Greek cities, and so called Ionic. Not only do the columns differ in appearance, and, for much of the Classical period, proportion, but they support different forms of entablature: Compare figure 14 with figure 21 (see below, Chapter 2). Generally speaking, the survival of a fragment from column or entablature will be sufficient to determine whether a Classical Greek building is in the Doric or Ionic 'order'. The third of the orders, Corinthian, is in essentials a variant of Ionic, the difference being determined only by the form of the capital which crowns the column. If the capital is totally lost, the difference between Ionic and Corinthian cannot readily be determined. Corinthian, however, occurs very rarely for internal columns in Greek temples of the fourth century BC (one example is in the interior of the temple of Apollo at Bassae), and is not used externally for important buildings until the Hellenistic period. Even then it is still infrequent.

Reconstructing the elevation

To reconstruct an elevation, we must first determine the order. This will tell us the form of its columns and the succession of different elements in the entablature, and thus give us the essential information for a general conception of its appearance. This is not, in itself, enough. Although we can measure the size of the building in plan (and this book contains several examples of plans drawn to scale, which give an accurate impression of the relative size), plan dimensions do not in themselves give the vertical dimensions. We need to know the height of the columns employed, and the measurements of the various parts of the entablature. In the case of the temple of Hephaistos, these are all known elements; complete columns and all the parts of the entablature survive. It is these that give the present day appearance of the building, and they can be measured precisely. Even if they did not survive in their entirety, it would be simple to make a complete reconstruction drawing of the temple on the basis of the plan, two or three columns, and the section of entablature that comes over them. These elements do not have to be standing for a drawing to be made. Of the temple of Zeus at Olympia, only the platform and the lower sections of the walls still remain in their original positions, the rest having been overthrown in a violent earthquake in the sixth century AD. But much of the colonnade and enough of the entablature remains where it fell, and these pieces can be measured to give a drawing of them in their original form. Of other temples, less remains, and here there are problems of a different nature. The temple of Ares, the god of war, which had been built in the time of Perikles in that god's sanctuary at Acharnai, an outlying *deme* (village) to the north of Athens, was moved in the first century BC from its original site into the agora at Athens. It was re-erected on a solid mortared base, so that we do not have the lines of foundation which are the normal way of determining the plan of a demolished Greek temple. However, the base indicates the general size, and fragments of the superstructure are sufficient to show that it must have been essentially similar to the temple of Hephaistos, of similar date and, in all probability, the work of the same architect. But although fragments of the columns survive, they are not sufficient to give us the full column dimensions, and their height remains unknown. Comparison with the temple of Hephaistos and that of Poseidon at Sounion (which is again sufficiently similar in dimensions, plan and detail for it to be attributed to the same architect) gives us a range for the column height. Although Hephaistos and Poseidon are not absolutely identical, they suggest an approximate figure which can be used for reconstructing the temple of Ares. We cannot be sure of its accuracy, and this lack of accuracy must always be borne in mind when comparing this temple with others. But for most purposes, the guess will do (the height of the columns of Hephaistos is 5.713 m., of Poseidon 6.024 m. W.B. Dinsmoor's estimate for Ares is c. 6.275 m.).

This is a particularly easy example, when direct comparison can be made with other buildings which are very closely related. But even when this cannot be done, as in the case of Doric temples, provided we know the date, or approximate date at which it was built, we can determine the likely proportions, height compared with diameter, of its columns. In the sixth century BC columns are relatively stubby (short in comparison to their diameter), becoming more slender in the fifth century, and very slender in the fourth century and Hellenistic periods. Their capitals, too, change proportions in the course of time, early ones being flat and shallow, like saucers; then becoming steeper sided and heavier; declining in size compared with the length of the shaft in the fifth and later centuries. Again, reconstruction of the precise form requires the survival of at least a significant fragment of the original. Other proportions are more variable: the entablature of the temple of Hephaistos, for example, proportionate to the columns, is relatively higher than that of its exact contemporary and neighbour, the Parthenon.

The ability to reconstruct accurately, then, depends on the quality and quantity of surviving information; and in judging reconstruction drawings of Classical buildings, it is always necessary to check the details of the information on which they are based. Since the information is more likely to be complete (or completable) for the plan than for the elevation, it is more usual in books on Greek architecture to find individual buildings illustrated by plan rather than elevation. To appreciate these buildings it is necessary for the reader to reconstruct in the mind's eye the elevation; to look at the plan and see the columns (what sort of column, how tall they were) standing on the plan as on a base; and then to see everything that would come over them, in accordance with the regular patterns to which Greek buildings conform.

Stock forms

Regularity of pattern, the repetition of standard form, makes this relatively easy for Greek architecture. It is never the role of the architect to invent new forms or to make his name by imposing idiosyncratic design on the work he is undertaking. His job is to supervise, to see that everything is properly constructed; he designs strictly within predetermined limits. Relative proportions, the relationship between one element of a design and another is determined by precedent; they may be modified, but the modification has to develop from what has been done previously. Even though Iktinos, the architect of the Parthenon, succeeds in imposing on that building a series of harmonies based on the relationship 4:9 ($2^2:3^2$), the Parthenon itself resembles in its essential arrangements other temples of the same period (or, indeed, those of a previous century).

So the understanding of ancient Greek buildings means that their type, their context must be recognized, as much as any idiosyncrasies they may possess. There is, in fact, a limited number of stock forms, and it is very simple to recognize the general category of building (and so its purpose and function) from the plan. Besides the vernacular houses, the main categories are those of religious architecture, and civic architecture – the administrative and other buildings of the city. These two categories were not as separated in ancient Greek cities as they are at the present day. Theatres and athletic stadiums, which today are concerned with purely secular activities, in ancient Greece were very much part of the religious system: plays and athletic contests belonged to the cult of the relevant gods. Even the civic administration took place in buildings which were normally provided with altars for sacrifices to the gods, or which were adjacent to shrine buildings.

Temples were the most important buildings. The gods, and fear of the gods, dominated the Classical cities – the importance of religion in daily life was closer to that of the middle ages than to present day secular society. So the temples came first, as pleasing to the gods. It is in the temples, as we shall see, that the forms of Greek architecture developed; the orders, Doric and Ionic, were invented to make them more splendid. The same orders were used (or simplified wooden systems substituted) for the extended stoas or porticoes, which provided shelter in the sanctuaries, and also, very frequently, in other parts of the Greek city.

Houses and the use of enclosed space

Vernacular buildings – the houses – are generally less well built, and so do not survive above the stone footings on which their mudbrick walls stood (well preserved houses, with stone walls, are rare and the result of special circumstances – on Delos, for example, in the Hellenistic period, where stone was more cheaply available than mudbrick). There are two main types, important for the influence – in terms of traditional form – which they have on the more important public buildings. The earlier houses, of the eighth century, say, are often only simple huts, roughly rectangular, though perhaps with slightly curved rather than straight walls. Where they stand as isolated buildings, and especially if they are given porches at one end, they resemble the essential room and porch of a temple. In this sense, the temple is the house of the god, embellished beyond the levels appropriate to the house of humans, but similarly a building standing isolated in space. But, more often, houses came to consist of a series of hut-like rooms grouped together, and at some stage the idea was extended to group them round a courtyard: instead of standing as an isolated structure surrounded by space, the building itself encloses space. This introduced a new architectural principle. It cannot be used for temples, since their form is already fixed, and religious conservatism will not allow it to be modified; but the idea of defining the space within a sanctuary by surrounding it with stoas is eventually found. Enclosing space with surrounding colonnades is, however, used for other purposes: exercise grounds (gymnasia) and the schools which were attached to them; and meeting places for special groups of people, where privacy is required. The function of these is often best understood from the rooms built behind the colonnade, where it is possible to discern their purpose. Some contained tiers of seats, arranged as in a theatre, but seating a far smaller number – meeting places for restricted political bodies, the councils (*boulai*). Others have rooms which once contained the couches on which Greeks reclined for feasting, and so are formal banqueting halls. Similar rooms, though, may be found behind single stoas, or among the rooms of a private house.

Although details of embellishment may vary, a striking feature of Greek architecture is its universality within the Greek world, from the colonies of Sicily and Italy to the cities of Asia Minor. Only in the Hellenistic age, when Greek settlement was extended far afield into areas with non-Greek architectural traditions can we see new forms developing. These, however, are generally limited to the new areas, Egypt, for example, or Bactria, while the Greek heartland remained true to established practice.

Chapter 2
The Early Development of Classical Temples

Dark Age beginnings

During the late Bronze Age, in the period down to about 1200 BC, the rulers of Mycenaean Greece had put up buildings of real architectural quality: the Palaces from which they organized and administered their kingdoms, and the tombs in which they were buried. These buildings show a combination of influences: from vernacular tradition, and from other civilizations (most immediately, that of Minoan Crete) with which the Mycenaeans were in contact. Other buildings – including religious shrines – were built more in accordance with vernacular forms. The Royal Architecture was linked inextricably with the dominant political system and when, for whatever reason, this collapsed in the twelfth century BC, the related architecture ceased. In the succeeding 'Dark' age, only vernacular buildings were constructed. The archaeological evidence is scanty in the extreme, but there are increasing signs that one of the building types employed was the long but rather narrow hut, with a porch entrance at one end, and side walls that form the shape of an elongated horseshoe. All that survives of them are the rubble footings on which their mudbrick walls were placed, and (in the larger examples) the holes in which the wooden posts to support the roof stood. The roofs themselves were thatched.

By far the most impressive of these Dark Age buildings was that discovered recently at Lefkandi in Euboea, over 45 m. in length, and some 10 m. wide. It seems to have been built to mark a sumptuous burial, purely for display, and it was made even more magnificent, in size if not in material, by the addition of an external colonnade of wooden posts. It dates to the tenth century BC; and so anticipated a similar horseshoe building at Thermon in Aetolia (western Greece), which was subsequently demolished and covered with a temple dedicated to Apollo. The building at Lefkandi seems to have had a short life, perhaps not more than 50 years or so. There is nothing else known from the Dark Age which can be defined as architectural in quality.

Origins of the Classical temple

The real beginnings of Classical architecture belong to the time, in the late eighth and seventh century BC, when we can trace the first recognizable development of the Classical city states. Belief in the Olympian deities must have existed before this time, and they must have been worshipped, but there is really no architectural evidence for it – certainly no buildings that can be recognized as temples. During the eighth century we begin to find buildings which, though still vernacular in style and construction, are definitely dedicated to religious cult – the small horseshoe-shaped buildings at Eretria and Perachora, for example, and even more interesting, the terracotta model of such a building, apparently given as an offering to Hera at her Perachora sanctuary. Why the Greeks should begin to develop recognizable religious sanctuaries during this period is obscure, and we can only speculate about the causes. But the earliest temples seem to have followed the vernacular house forms of the Dark Age: in other words, what is being built is simply a special house for the god. By this time the great tomb building at Lefkandi was long since buried and forgotten; it cannot, in itself, have influenced temple form. Yet with its surrounding colonnade of wooden posts it looks uncannily like a Classical peripteral temple. The wealth of the Lefkandi burial demonstrates that it belongs to persons we might term a king and his queen. The implication is that the building in which they were placed after death resembled that in which they resided when they were alive; that powerful people in important places had particularly magnificent homes, marked out by the addition of external colonnades of wooden posts. Unfortunately, no evidence for such houses has yet been found.

Other possible sources of inspiration for the Classical temple may be sought outside Greece. In the Near East there is a continuing tradition of constructing temples to the gods, running unbroken from the Late Bronze Age. Solomon's temple in Jerusalem is undoubtedly part of this sequence, and there were countless others, some of which have been excavated. Some of them, such as one at Tell Ta'ayanat in Syria, have a strong resemblance to the smaller, non-peripteral Greek temples. The fact that recognizable temples to the gods began to be found in Greece during the eighth century BC, which is the time when some Greek cities and their traders began to establish closer links with the cities of the Near East, strongly suggests Eastern inspiration in the concept of the temple, and at least an Eastern contribution to its form. But this does not seem to have included the surrounding colonnade. If other forms of Greek art of this period are considered, particularly sculpture, we can detect a similar phenomenon. Early Greek stone statues, the *Kouroi*, show a strong Egyptian influence, but they are not merely copies of Egyptian sculpture; instead, they introduce traits (particularly in the form of the head) that are more likely to be derived from a Greek tradition of carving in wood. There is, in fact, no simple origin for the Classical Greek temple. A word of caution is necessary at this point. The basic room of the developed Greek temple with its end porch strongly resembles in plan the principal room of the Mycenaean palaces, to which modern scholars have given the Homeric term *megaron*. Thus, it is suggested that the Classical temple derives from the *megaron* of the Mycenaean palace. This is, in fact, highly improbable. The Mycenaean palaces were all destroyed by the twelfth century BC, and there is an interval of at least four centuries before the first construction of temples, a gap which rules out any question of a direct link. Nor is there any real evidence that the Mycenaean *megaron* and the early temples had the same function. More likely, both are comparable derivatives of the vernacular hut form.

The temple form emerges

By the middle of the seventh century BC, at least in the more progressive cities of Greece, that is, those which were most closely involved overseas, particularly with the Near East, a clear idea of the prestigious form of the temple was emerging. Size was a significant factor: the temple should be a 'hundred footer', a *hekatompedon*. It is now rectangular, rather than horseshoe-shaped in plan. It has an inner room – a cella – with a porch, but still likely to be narrow in proportion, like the building at Lefkandi. Most importantly, it is peripteral, surrounded by a rectangle of posts which enhance its external appearance. It employs superior methods of construction, with better materials, and – although the direct evidence is scanty – it is now given decorative treatment, particularly on the exterior. It is during this evolution that the forms of the Greek orders of architecture, Doric and Ionic, develop. In terms of actual survival, Doric and Ionic are not recognizable until the early years of the sixth century BC or the preceding decade or so. But from this time onward one or other style is normal in Greek buildings of any pretensions as architecture. Now the columns are stone, and so are the different elements of the entablature. The walls, too, are built from blocks of stone and though wood is still retained for the supporting framework of the roof, the roof itself is now constructed, not of thatch but from tiles, generally of baked clay.

The Doric order

Yet the forms of decoration, and the different elements in the entablature are inexplicable in terms of stone construction; and it is generally agreed that in fact they present concepts originally achieved in wood. This is particularly noticeable in the entablature of the Doric order. In its standard, developed form this comprises three elements: the main beam or architrave which is supported directly by the columns; then, over this, a frieze; and finally, over the frieze a projecting cornice, or *geison*. The function of the *geison* is to throw the rain that falls on the roof clear of the vertical structure underneath (few Doric buildings have gutters – *simas* – over the cornice, and even when gutters are used, they are pierced at intervals by spouts, usually decorated in the form of lions' heads which allow the rainwater to run out at cornice level). All three elements, as figures 13 and 14 show, are decorated. The architrave has a projecting band, or *tainia* running along its top edge, and this is punctuated at regular intervals on its underside by additional rectangular blocks (the *regulae*) with projecting 'drops' or *guttae*, along their under surface. The frieze also is decorated, as an alternation of two elements, flat square slabs or *metopes*, separated by upright rectangular elements, called the *triglyphs*, divided into three vertical strips by intervening grooves. The *regulae* on the architrave are positioned so that they come directly under the triglyphs. The sloping undersurface of the *geison* is also decorated with rectangular blocks, the *mutules* carrying rows of *guttae*. These are placed over the triglyphs, and also over the intervening metopes.

All these decorative elements are normally carved, in each of the three sections, on the same blocks of stone, placed in sequence. However, in some of the more important buildings the metopes are made from separate slabs of stone, which are slotted into place between the projecting edges of adjacent triglyphs (this is particularly true of buildings such as the Parthenon where the metopes are decorated with sculpture in relief). Yet it seems that they originally represented the fitting together of different wooden elements. The architrave would then have consisted of baulks of timber, surmounted perhaps by a continuous and projecting plank (the *tainia*). The triglyphs on top of this would also have been timber blocks, fixed to the architrave beams by wooden dowels driven upwards into them through the plank-*tainia*. The stone *guttae* then represent these wooden dowels. Similarly, the mutules with their dowel-*guttae* served to fix the rafters of the roof to the overhanging cornice.

Where uncertainty arises is in the original form and purpose of the frieze, and in particular in the very curious form of the triglyphs. A favourite explanation is that they represent the ends of horizontal beams, supporting the roof and resting on the architrave, the metopes simply being used to fill the intervening spaces. But there are considerable difficulties with this. It does not explain the peculiar grooved form which gives the triglyphs (triple grooves) their name. Alhough no actual wooden beams survive from classical architecture, there is enough evidence for their shape (the holes in the stonework into which they were fitted) to show that they were invariably squared in section, not rectangular. Yet triglyphs are invariably rectangular. Finally, in Doric peripteral buildings, where triglyph and metope friezes meet at right angles, at the corners, there is a very firm rule that each frieze should end with a triglyph. This means that triglyphs should be adjacent to each other at right angles, where they cannot possibly represent beam ends, since it is not possible to place beams to meet at right angles in this way. The solution must be more complex. The original forms are undoubtedly achieved in wood, but they are more the result of applied decoration than simple structural necessity. Thus the sequence of triglyphs and metopes is in origin a decorative pattern, designed to enhance appearance so that the buildings – certainly temples – in which this was first done were the first examples of conscious and deliberate architectural design. To demonstrate this, given that the original evidence does not survive, it is necessary to prove the decorative nature of the frieze. We cannot assign a precise date but it must have happened between the time of the temples at Perachora and Eretria of the mid eighth century BC (to which the application of this decorated form is a structural impossibility), and the earliest material evidence for it, the terracotta metope slabs, of about 625 BC used to decorate the temple of Apollo at Thermon, but made (as the form of the clay and the painted decoration on them proves) at Corinth. The decorative pattern of alternating squares and rectangles, the rectangles divided into (normally) three vertical bands, is in fact a commonplace at this time. It occurs on Greek vases in the geometric style made in Athens in the

Fig. 6. 'Triglyph and metope' pattern (with other patterns also found on Greek buildings) from a Cypriot vase of the seventh century BC.

eighth century BC, as well as on other vases of the same or slightly later date elsewhere, particularly in Cyprus. It is also found as a decorative pattern on works of art – ivories, for example – made in the Syrian/Phoenician cities. It is a straightforward – but momentous – development to run this same motif as a decorative pattern round the upper part of temple buildings.

The Ionic order

The forms of the Ionic order are similarly a mixture of structure and decoration. There is less consistency in the details, and it is not until the Hellenistic period that any real uniformity is achieved. The column is more slender, in the Classical period, than Doric. Where the shaft of the Doric column is placed directly on the stylobate, the Ionic has its own base, decorated in different ways, which seem to depend on local preferences. Like Doric the shaft is normally decorated with a series of vertical flutings, but these are much narrower in proportion to their height than on a Doric column. Whereas the thicker Doric shaft normally has only twenty, the more slender Ionic has twenty-four, and while the Doric have only a sharp edge of stone between them, Ionic are separated by a flatter band.

The effect of this is to heighten the impression of slenderness. The capital is completely different: where Doric has a circular spreading element (the *echinus*) supporting a square bearing surface (the *abacus*), Ionic is decorated with conspicuous pairs of volutes. The Ionic entablature has, like Doric, three parts, but they differ in form. The architrave is normally decorated with three bands (*fasciae*) each projecting a little further than that below, while the Doric *tainia* is replaced by a continuous moulded band. Over this comes a frieze – in east Greek examples, a series of small projecting blocks (dentils) which do look like the ends of small beams. In Athens these are replaced by a continuous band, usually decorated with sculpture. Above this the cornice or *geison* does not have the mutules of the Doric version, and is of slightly differing profile. Thus Ionic shares with Doric a common structural purpose, but receives decoration from a different source. The principal influence is quite clear. Volute, or 'lily' capitals are a commonplace in the architecture of the Near East, where they already existed in some abundance before the eighth century and the development of Greek contact with this area. They are, therefore, a direct borrowing. Some of the Greek capitals are essentially the same as the Near Eastern version, with separate volutes springing from a central triangle. They are found in the North East Aegean area, the 'Aeolic' region, and are often called by that name to distinguish them from Ionic. They die out in the early fifth century BC. The true Ionic capital modifies the eastern form by linking the two volutes across the top of a decorated *echinus*.

The early temples

The earliest substantial temples seem to belong to the early part of the seventh century BC (the first peripteral temple dedicated to Hera on the island of Samos may be as early as the eighth). None of them can be assigned on the evidence of the surviving architecture to one or other of the orders. However, it is reasonable to suppose that if their wooden superstructures had survived they would be recognizable as Doric or Ionic, depending on their geographical locality. For Doric, a very important early temple is that of Poseidon at the Isthmus of Corinth. This survived until the time of Xerxes' invasion of Greece, when it was destroyed and replaced by a new temple in the same position. The original had to be dismantled completely and its plan was rediscovered, mostly in the form of robbed foundation trenches; but some quantity of the dismantled material remained and was collected together in the modern excavations. The early temple had a two-stepped base, on which stood wooden columns supporting a wooden entablature, all trace of which is therefore lost. The roof was of terracotta tiles. Surviving examples show that, unlike later temples which invariably had pediments at the ends, this roof sloped down to the front and rear as well as the sides of the surrounding colonnade (i.e. it had a 'hipped' roof). The cella walls were built from squared blocks of stone, this being presumably the easiest part to build in stone rather than the traditional materials. Blocks of it have been pieced together, and show that the wall was decorated with a series of panels, apparently copying a massive timber framework with mudbrick infill. We can see here the beginning of the conversion of timber and mudbrick to stone construction. The temple of Hera at Olympia, which is at least fifty years later in date (around 590 BC) shows no advance in technique, and its walls had only a raised footing in stone; but in this building, which survived through to the Late Roman period, the original wooden columns were replaced in stone piecemeal at widely different dates and so to widely variable proportions. These are however all Doric, and suggest that both the wooden columns they replace, and the wooden entablature they supported, were already Doric in form. The early temples of Hera on the island of Samos were essentially similar in construction, with wooden columns and entablature, but being in the East Greek area were presumably Ionic in form, as, of course, were their stone successors.

Stone temples

The changeover to stone construction introduced a new range of techniques to Greek building. Their development coincides with the substantial opening up of Egypt to Greek traders, mercenary soldiers and settlers, which revealed to the Greeks a far more massive form of architecture than that of the Near Eastern communities – one which was dependent on stone construction, with stone rather than wooden columns. The basic techniques of stone architecture were undoubtedly learnt by the Greeks in Egypt. The application of these techniques begins in the quarries. There is no particular difficulty, in the limestone and marble regions of Greece, in quarrying building blocks, and the temple at Isthmia shows that this begins relatively early on. Larger blocks were needed for the entablature, and this remained wooden in the temple of Hera at Olympia, because the local stone was inferior in quality. However, at about the same time, large entablature blocks were quarried for the temple of Artemis at Corfu. More complex were the columns. In later Greek temples of any size columns were built up from drums dowelled together, but in earlier temples column shafts were made of single blocks of stone. The temple of Aphaia on the island of Aigina, built early in the fifth century BC, is the last major temple with monolithic column shafts – some five metres in length. Quarrying large blocks of stone is commonplace in Egypt. In Greece, the same technique was needed for the colossal blocks of stone from which statues were made, and it is significant that the development of stone sculpture coincides with the development of stone as the building material for temples.

Stoneworking techniques

Equally laborious was the transport of building stone from the quarry to the construction site. Wherever possible, this was done by sea (the marble quarries of Paros and Naxos are at an advantage in being close to the sea), but some building sites were inland, and transport in ox-drawn wagons was necessary. Quite clearly, Greek technology in the sixth century was able to cope with this since building stone (including Naxian and Parian marble) was taken from the harbours in the Gulf of Itea inland and uphill to the sanctuary at Delphi. To obviate the risk of damage, building blocks would normally be trimmed only roughly to size in the quarry, the surfaces being hammered to the right dimensions. The final work was carried out at the building site, and the evidence for this frequently survives in the layers of stone chippings – the debris of stone carving – which are spread around the temples. Pliny tells us that column shafts were turned on a lathe, a technique invented by Theodoros, one of the architects of the first stone temple of Hera at Samos. This sounds complicated, given the colossal weight of monolithic shafts, but would be a relatively simple way of cutting the shaft to the required profile, which, in Doric particularly, was given a curve (entasis) often very pronounced in the sixth century BC, less so in later temples. When columns were made up from drums these were usually quarried in circular drum form (there are examples of half quarried column drums still left in the quarries which produced the marble for the temple of Poseidon at Sounion: see figure 20).

During construction the stones were worked more finely, but in the workshop only those surfaces which were to come into direct

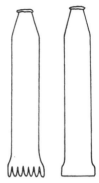

Fig. 7. Flat bladed and toothed chisels.

contact with other blocks, or were to act as a reference point for the final form, were completely finished; otherwise an unfinished surface was left, to protect the block from accidental damage during construction. Contact surfaces are kept to a minimum. To reduce the amount of accurate preparation required, blocks were often slightly hollowed at the ends to avoid direct contact. Surfaces were prepared by chisel, and a development in stoneworking technique can be seen in the buildings of the sixth century BC. At first, stonemasons used only a flat-bladed chisel, which leaves a series of striations on the block being worked. Later, a chisel with a toothed blade (a claw chisel) was developed, particularly for marble, which may shatter under the impact of a flat-bladed chisel. At Delphi, the use of the claw chisel seems to have been introduced around 525 BC by masons from the island of Naxos, who worked blocks of marble supplied from that island – though Naxian marble had been used much earlier for Ionic buildings at Delos. The final surfaces were prepared by rubbing and polishing after the building was complete. In some unfinished buildings, this stage was never achieved. Blocks were lifted by block and tackle and rope, and placed close to their final position; they were then moved into this with the aid of crowbars.

In important buildings, blocks were fixed to each other. Wooden clamps had been used for this in Egyptian architecture, and similar clamps are found in Greek buildings of the sixth century BC (see fig. 8 which shows how they got their name, 'butterfly' clamps). Later Greek architects devised the more durable form of iron clamps, fixed into the upper surfaces of blocks by means of molten lead. More interesting are the dowels used to peg blocks in place. A not dissimilar

Fig. 8. Clamp holes, early fifth-century apsidal building at Emporio, Chios.

dowelling technique was employed in fixing together ships' timbers (it has been found, for example, in the surviving timbers of the Kyrenia wreck, and has been used with complete success in the reconstruction of the Athenian trireme). Here we seem to have a wood-working technique adapted, like the architectural form, to stone buildings, and explaining why the word for a designer of buildings *architekton* (the origin, of course, of our word architect), means 'master carpenter'.

Architectural design

Design also was a matter of accepted tradition and only gradual, or minor, modification. The most startling and sudden innovations must have belonged to the revolutionary buildings of the seventh century BC, for the construction of stone architecture is essentially based on the acceptance (and so imitation) of established forms. The methods of design are never described for the early or Classical period (the instructions in Vitruvius seem to derive from little earlier than the second century BC). Egyptian artists know how to make scale drawings on squared papyrus, but Greek architects seem to have proceeded rather by rule of thumb – laying out the full dimensions of the building on the site, and proceeding from this to work out the size of the next stage: from foundations to steps, from steps to the arrangement of column spacing and column diameters. From this can be calculated the column height, according to the accepted proportions of the time, and from the columns the desired arrangement of the entablature. This simple procedure must explain several apparent peculiarities in Greek architecture: that in the construction of temples, for example, external colonnades are erected, including the entablature, before any work is carried out on the interior walls. This is despite the obvious fact that to carry and lift blocks of building stone through an already erected colonnade risks accident and damage. The reason must be that the arrangement, and particularly the height, of the walls is determined by that of the colonnade, which cannot be 'read' in advance from a scale plan. Another more specific oddity: the temples of Hephaistos by the Athenian agora, Poseidon at Sounion, and Ares formerly at Acharnai are all so similar that it has been plausibly argued that they are by the same architect, and to the same design. Yet they all vary slightly from each other, in minor modifications of dimensions, and similarity is more readily observed in proportion, rather than linear measurement. In other words, they were built by the same procedures, but not taken from a single predetermined plan.

'The lack of innovation'

This also explains the lack of innovation in Greek architecture. The principle of construction is that of vertical supports and horizontal beams. Architrave blocks are supported at each end on a column, and the roofs depend on wooden beams which rest on the entablature, the walls, and, in large buildings, internal colonnades. This limited technique restricts the dimensions of buildings. Stone architraves have to be built from blocks which span from column to column, so that the Parthenon has to use massive blocks over $4^{1}/_{2}$ metres in length. To facilitate construction, the Parthenon architrave is built of three series of blocks, one to the front, another forming the back, and a third block sandwiched between. Indeed, all but the smallest temples of the Classical period find it desirable to use two lines of blocks. This limits the spacing of the columns, and it is exceptional to find anything much larger than this. Most are much smaller. Equally restricting is the application of this principle to the wooden beams. Greek architecture generally did not build up its roof supports by complex carpentry (such as the hammer beam roofs of medieval architecture). The wider the space, the more massive the beam required, but there was a limit to the size of available timbers. In general, Greek architects could not use beams longer than about 12 metres. More massive timbers may have been available to architects in Macedonia (the source of Athenian ship timber) but Greek roofs nowhere attain the considerable span of Roman buildings, whose carpentry techniques were more sophisticated. Macedonian architects probably invented and certainly developed stone barrel vaulting; but because it differed from normal roofing systems it was largely restricted to tombs buried and concealed underground.

Building costs

Major buildings were expensive. Accurate calculations of the actual cost of temples are not really possible. Some building accounts of expenditure were inscribed on stone, in fifth-century Athens and fourth-century Epidauros, but they are not always complete. Even so, we can see that the cost of the Parthenon was comparable with the annual income from the Athenian Empire, while construction of the Tholos at Epidauros was spread over a long period of time, and was actually interrupted because of a shortage of funds. Greek cities were prepared to spend very large sums of money (compared with their revenues) to honour the gods. The sources of revenue varied. Some sanctuaries raised money themselves. Delphi and Epidauros organized collections to pay for their fourth-century buildings. Wealthy individuals might help: Cleisthenes made a major contribution to the sixth century temple at Delphi. Funds belonging to the cities were used; indemnities were imposed on defeated enemies; fines were collected from individual transgressors. Careful checks were imposed to see that money was properly spent, the materials purchased sound, and the workmanship carried out to the desired standard. Wealthy individuals, as a service to the city and the god, would take on the role of guarantors, promising to pay from their own resources for anything that was not well done. This gave them the incentive to see that everything was carried out properly, in addition to the duties and obligations imposed on the architect.

The architects

The architects themselves had to be masters not only of design, which they could learn only by something akin to an apprenticeship system – there were no schools of architecture in Classical Greece – but also masters of the techniques employed. In a society which often distinguished sharply between landed wealth and earning one's living through labour – to the detriment of the latter – there are obvious arguments for putting architects in the lower class. The salary of Theodotos, architect of the temple of Asklepios at Epidauros, is recorded in the building inscriptions: he gets 353 drachmai for the year, little more than the wage of a labourer. Yet many architects' names are known and recorded, and they often appear to have been substantial members of society. So perhaps the payment is only to cover living expenses, and the architect works from a sense of obligation – the duty system which is fundamental to the functioning of the Greek city state. Clearly, he was not tied to one city. His skills were in demand, and architects are found who work in different places. The same is true of the craftsmen, and they must have been prepared to travel where work was available, for it was rare for cities to run continuous programmes of public construction. Skilled non-Athenians are listed amongst the craftsmen who worked on the Erechtheion, as are slaves; but these are slaves purchased for their skills, not just as cheap labour. It is wrong to regard Greek buildings as the product of a slave based economy, and dependent, therefore, on slavery.

The skills of Greek architects and their craftsmen developed in the course of the sixth century BC, and there is some flexibility in the working pattern. At Delphi, for example, it would seem that local craftsmen built, in about 525 BC, out of local stone, the base on which the Treasury of the Siphnians was constructed; but, as we have seen, workmen from Naxos or Paros must have been taken to Delphi to construct the marble superstructure of the building. Nevertheless, in the archaic period and later, much architecture was locally based, and though craftsmen were generally not restricted to a single city, there was often enough work for them within a defined area. Consequently local patterns of architectural form do develop, as a result of local experience being uninfluenced by other regions, and because local designs adapt their procedures to the requirements of locally available material. In the sixth century, for example, there is a distinctive style of Doric temple in Sicily. There are links between different buildings in the Peloponnese – a whole series of temples in the Argolid and adjacent regions which share certain features. In the sixth century the Ionic of Samos and Ephesus and Miletus differs in detail from that of Chios and at the same time they all differ from the

Ionic of the Cycladic islands. To the uninitiated, all Greek temples look alike. In fact, within the established traditions and forms, a large range of subtle variation is possible, and this is part of the fascination of Greek architecture.

Fig. 9. Temple of 'Concord', Akragas.

Chapter 3
Temples of the Classical Period

Fig. 10. Temple of Aphaia, Aigina.

The temple of Aphaia

The temple of Aphaia – a local equivalent of Artemis – at the north-eastern tip of the island of Aigina serves to represent the transition from the Archaic period to the fully Classical styles of the fifth century BC. The present building (which is quite heavily restored) replaces a smaller temple, built early in the sixth century and destroyed by fire somewhere around 500 BC. The new temple was larger and more impressive, peripteral, where the earlier one had columns only in its porch. Although the exact date of its construction is uncertain, recent excavations have produced, in association with the chips of stone that represent the period of building work, quantities of pottery of the first decades of the fifth century. A curiosity of the completed temple is that the sets of sculpture from its pediments (both of which depict the same subject, Greeks against Trojans) differ in style: that from the west pediment being related more to the Archaic style of the sixth century; that from the more important east pediment looking forward to the early Classsical style of about the time of Xerxes' invasion of Greece. To complicate matters, fragments (heads) of another set of Archaic style pediment figures have been found, apparently from sculpture removed from the temple and set up separately in the sanctuary area. It is difficult to reconcile all these chronological indications. However, it would appear that work on the temple (which fixes the date of its design) began as soon as its predecessor was destroyed, though there may well have been some delay down to the time of the Persian Wars before it was complete.

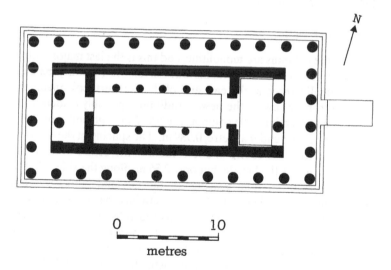

0   10

metres

Fig. 11. Plan, temple of Aphaia, Aigina.

Dimensions and platform of the temple

The temple stands on a three-stepped base, the form which had emerged as normal for Doric temples in Mainland Greece by the end of the sixth century. The steps, and in fact, all the superstructure of the temple except for its sculpture are of limestone, though most of the building was given a coating of thin hard stucco to create the impression of superior material. The overall dimensions – measured on the outer edge of the upper step, the stylobate – are 13.77 x 28.815 metres, which is not particularly large; indeed, it is similar in size to the temple of Hephaistos at Athens, 13.708 x 31.769 m., but substantially smaller than the Parthenon, 30.88 x 69.503 m.. On this stylobate was erected a colonnade of six columns across the ends and twelve columns along the sides. Thus the proportions of width to length are in the region of 1:2. Compared with other Doric temples, Aphaia is relatively short in proportion to its width. The platform is approached by a ramp, as this is found in other Doric temples of the Peloponnese (such as that of Zeus at Olympia, where the conventional division of the base into three steps gives step heights which are excessive for practical purposes). Ramps provided easy and dignified access, particularly for formal processions, on to the platform of the temple.

Spacing of columns

Most of the columns are monolithic, and this is the last major temple in Greece to be built with columns made in this sixth-century manner. Exceptionally, three at the east end of the northern colonnade are built up from drums, in the newer tradition – possibly evidence for delay in construction. The columns are 5.272 m. high and most have a diameter of just under a metre, 0.989 m. The spacing of the columns (measured from the centre of one column to the centre of the next) is 2.618 m. across the facade, but only 2.56 m. along the sides. In the sixth century differential spacing for facades and flanks was not infrequent: the temple of Apollo at Corinth has spacing of 4.028 and 3.744 m. respectively. In the fifth century the difference is minimized: Hephaistos at Athens has spacing of 2.583 and 2.581 m., the Parthenon 4.2965 and 4.2915 m. But these temples are longer in comparison with their width. The restricted flank space of Aphaia is, in part, a device made necessary by the desire to shorten the length of the temple. The proportion of the shaft gives it a height 5 $\frac{1}{3}$ times its lower diameter, a little on the heavy side (Hephaistos is 5 $\frac{2}{3}$) and again a legacy of sixth century taste; so, too, are the relatively heavy capitals, with large, steep-sided *echinus*.

The triglyph problem

Like all peripteral Doric temples of any size, Aphaia demonstrates the problem caused by the rule that each frieze must end with a triglyph, which conflicts at the corners with a second rule that triglyphs must always be centred either directly over the column or the intervening space. As a rough and ready guide, the architrave and the frieze of Doric temples are each equivalent in height to the diameter of the column and the width of the abacus at the top of the capital. Since the triglyph has to be rectangular rather than square, its width is considerably less than its height, and thus also less than the width of the abacus. The outer edge of the end triglyph, if centred on the end column, would be placed some distance in from the outer end of the abacus, and if this was (by our first rule) also the end of the frieze, the column and its capital would have to project some way beyond its end (see fig. 14). This was regarded as ugly; and a better balance is achieved by moving the end of the entablature, with its end triglyph, further out so that it more nearly corresponds to the outer corner of the abacus. But this means moving the triglyph away from its centre position over the end column. Greek architects therefore had to accept the need to break the rule of centrality in order to create a satisfactory appearance for the temple. This device brought other problems. If the next triglyph obeyed the rule of centrality, there would be an abnormally wide gap between it and the corner triglyph, and the metope used to fill the gap would therefore be rectangular rather than square. More adjustment was necessary. The next triglyph also was moved outwards, to lessen the distortion; and for the same reason the corner column was made slightly thicker, and also moved inwards, closer to its neighbours (at Aphaia the corner column has a diameter of 1.01 m., and the spacing from its neighbours is reduced to 2.40 m.).

All this juggling with the measurements is something achieved by the architect from experience, and the measuring out of the available space for the colonnades on the stepped base. It is too complicated a calculation for the limited practicalities of Greek arithmetic (which does not have decimal numerical symbols, or a proper understanding of fractions) to achieve on a scale drawing. Nowhere is the need for practical training and experience in Greek architecture more clearly demonstrated. Later architects – particularly those brought up in the different traditions of Ionic – regarded Doric as hopelessly flawed as an architectural style, and for this reason unsuitable for temples.

The cella of Aphaia

The cella of Aphaia was constructed after the colonnade was complete, and is a good example of conventional Doric form. The side walls are in alignment with the second and fifth columns of the facade, but the ends are totally unrelated to the side columns. There is a fairly deep porch at the east end, with two Doric columns between the antae (the decorated termination of the side walls); over these was a Doric entablature, running from anta to anta. The cella is divided, like a church, into a nave and side aisles by internal colonnades, elements of which have survived and have been re-erected with the aid of some modern replacement. As in most Doric temples which have this internal division – not all do – the inner colonnades are arranged as two storeys: a lower line of columns supporting a simple architrave, on which an upper row of smaller columns is directly superimposed. This system serves two purposes. It enables the cella ceiling to be placed at a reasonable height without having excessively large columns (columns the size of – or, as they would have to be, larger than – those of the exterior would take up too much of the interior space). The other possibility is that a side gallery can be supported on the middle architrave. This was certainly done at Aphaia – there are the traces of the slots into which beams were fitted – but it may well have been an afterthought rather than part of the original building. At the west end of the cella is another porch, similar to that at the east end but not so deep. This is again a normal feature of peripteral (but not of non-peripteral) Doric temples, in which it is generally a false porch for apparently decorative purposes only since it did not have a door leading into the cella. At Aphaia, however, a door was later opened – off centre, to take advantage of the jointing of the wall blocks – into the cella. The reason for this alteration and, probably, the addition of the internal gallery is emphasized by the clear traces which exist for metal grilles, closing the spaces between the facade columns. Temples were always places in which valuable offerings to the god were deposited (we have part of the ancient inventories of the Parthenon, and they included abundant objects of gold and silver). Aigina, until the independent city state was suppressed by the Athenians, was a wealthy community, and Aphaia received her share. The conventional closed floor space of the temple was too small for it and extra space had to be devised. We have no idea what form her cult image took. In addition to the pediment sculpture there may have been relief decoration on the metopes, but not on those of the exterior entablature. As at Olympia, they would probably have been restricted to the entablature of the porches. There would also have been painted decoration. The evidence for this is much clearer on the fragments of the earlier temple, ruined and buried after a mere seventy years or so in the open air, than on the later temple which has been subject to weathering for two and a half millennia.

Fig. 12. View of ruins of temple of Zeus at Olympia.

The temple of Zeus at Olympia

The temple of Zeus at Olympia is by any reckoning one of the major Greek temples. Not only do we have substantial remains of the building itself – it is still impressive even in its completely ruined state – but a detailed account of the building by the Greek traveller and geographer Pausanias. Pausanias visited Olympia in the second century AD, when the temple was already some six hundred years old and had undoubtedly undergone extensive repairs. He tells us the architect was called Libon, and that he came from Elis. Nothing else is known about him. The occasion for building the temple was the creation and extension of the unified city state of Elis, which expanded in the late 470s to include the district of Olympia – previously part of a small independent city called Pisa. The temple was built from the proceeds of Elis' plundering of Pisa. It was probably complete by 458/7 when the Spartans attached to it a golden shield to commemorate their defeat of the Athenians at Tanagra. Pausanias' account – which may be mistaken in several respects – probably derives from information he obtained at Olympia at the time of his visit; it may be influenced by patriotic Elean distortions. The temple seems too important, and the significance of its sculptural decoration suggests something more than a purely local political event. Olympia is, after all, one of the two most important sanctuaries in mainland Greece – the other is Delphi – which have significance to all Greek cities, in particular to those of the Dorian Peloponnese and their West Greek colonies – cities once ruled by the descendants of Herakles (still ruled, in the case of Sparta) whose labours are depicted on the metopes of the two porches. The east pediment, which depicts the chariot race between Pelops and Oinomaos, the legendary antecedent for the Olympic games, has a particularly Peloponnesian context; whereas the west pediment, showing the battle between the Lapiths (aided by Theseus) and Centaurs, has distinct Athenian connections. (It is interesting to note that this scene was painted on the walls of the shrine in the Athenian agora in which, at this same period, Cimon had reburied the bones he believed to be the remains of Theseus.) Symbolically, the battle between Greeks and the beastly Centaurs stands for the struggle between the Greek cities and the Persian barbarians. Such a large temple, in such a place and at such a date, may well have been a thankoffering to Zeus by Sparta and her allies for deliverance from Persia – whatever Pausanias believed.

Dimensions, columns, sculptures

When it was first built, the temple was the largest in mainland Greece. It stands on a colossal three-stepped platform, 27.68 x 64.12 m. The steps are, of course, far too large to be of practical use, and the actual approach onto the platform, as at Aigina, is by way of a ramp. On this platform stood six by thirteen massive Doric columns; facade and flank spacing is virtually the same and the proportions of width to length, 1:2.316, more in accordance with fifth-century norm. The columns themselves are 10.43 m. high, and have a normal lower diameter of 2.21 m., or about 1 to 4³/₄. Thus they are thicker and clumsier than the columns of Aphaia, and appear more old-fashioned; the reason for this is undoubtedly the very inferior, shelly stone from which the temple was built. Good quality limestone, as

Fig. 13. Reconstruction drawing, temple of Zeus at Olympia.

used at Aphaia, was not locally available at Olympia, and the cost of transporting it from elsewhere was regarded as prohibitive. So the appearance of the temple had to be adjusted to allow for the poor quality of the stone. The entablature is equally massive, virtually half the height of the columns. A continuous gutter along the bottom of the roof would have served to emphasize even more this heaviness. The cella is arranged in the same way as that of Aphaia, though of course there is no door into it from the rear false porch. It was divided by internal colonnades, necessary in a temple of this size to support the roof. The magnificent pediment sculptures, in Parian marble, would have been the immediate focus of attention for the facades, and this may have distracted from the architectural shortcomings of the design. The external metopes were left plain, as at Aphaia (they were later adorned with captured shields by the Roman general Mummius, after the final conquest of Greece by the Romans in 146 BC); the sculptured metopes are those over the porches. The cult statue – described in detail by Pausanias – was Pheidias' masterpiece, the seated Zeus made from gold and ivory that was one of the seven wonders of the world. This was Pheidias' last work, and dates to the late 430s after he had been exiled from Athens. Its fame was due partly to its size, which was out of scale even with the large temple in which it was placed, for it was evident that if Zeus had risen from the throne on which he was seated his head would have gone through the roof. It does not seem that this was the original, or intended statue,

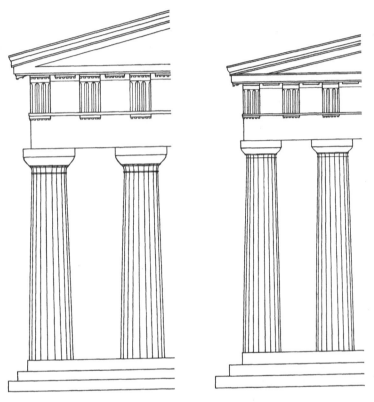

Fig. 14. Drawing to compare Doric order of Zeus Olympia with that of the Parthenon.

but was created later in a bid to outdo Pheidias' other great statue, that of Athena in the Parthenon.

Pentelic marble

In the late sixth century the Athenians began to work the marble quarries of Mt Pentelikos, on the east side of Attica. These produce a good quality stone, not as fine or purely white as the marble of Paros, but still completely suitable both for architecture and sculpture. Metopes of Pentelic marble were used in the final reconstruction, about 525 BC, of the temple of Athena on the Acropolis – the traditional or 'old' temple. After the defeat of the Persians at

Marathon in 490, the Athenians began to work on a quite massive programme of buildings in Pentelic marble, presumably as thankofferings. The only one completed was the small temple-like 'Treasury' at Delphi (see below, Chapter 5). At Athens itself, work started on a splendid new gateway building, a propylon on to the Acropolis, and a colossal temple. The latter was to be erected partly on massive substructures built along the south side of the Acropolis and to stand, therefore, by the side of the 'old' temple. Neither of these buildings was complete when the Persians returned, in 480, and damaged by fire what had been already achieved.

The Parthenon

After the Persian wars Athens and Sparta fell out; and in 451 or there-abouts the Athenians, who by now were challenging for the supremacy in Greece, considered it proper that they should build new temples both to commemorate their victory over Persia as well as to glorify the city and make its architectural splendour worthy of its status. Most

Fig. 15. Photograph of the Acropolis from Ardettos, taken by Stillman in 1869. This shows how the Acropolis and the Parthenon dominated the undeveloped nineteenth-century town of Athens, much as it did the ancient city.

important of these was the renewal of the plan to build a large temple to Athena on the Acropolis, which would dominate the city – something which can be more easily appreciated from nineteenth-century photographs of Athens than from the modern concrete sprawl of the Greek capital. It was clearly intended to be the most magnificent temple in Greece, and to outshine the Temple of Zeus at Olympia. The foundations of the Marathon temple were to be the starting point, since the costly and deep south foundations could not be replaced. But on the north side, where the Acropolis rock is higher and no deep foundations are necessary, the temple was extended. The original width was intended to be 23.533 m. Now the temple was extended to 30.88 m., and so wider than Zeus at Olympia. It was not so greatly extended in length – the original length, at 66.94 m. gave a surprisingly long and narrow structure, with six by sixteen columns. The new length, 69.503 m., accommodated one extra column, making a total of seventeen along the flank; but the facade now comprised eight instead of six, a ratio of width to length of 1 to $2^{1/4}$ – the equivalent of 4:9 – that is, 2^2 to 3^2, a mathematically 'significant' ratio which was deliberately chosen by the architect, and which recurs in other proportions of the building.

The temple, like its predecessor, was to be completely marble –

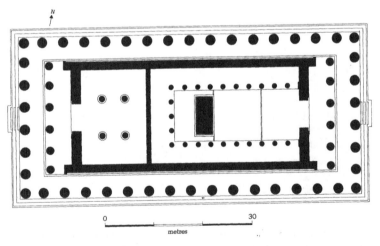

Fig. 16. Plan of the Parthenon.

even the tiles are made from massive and heavy marble slabs. The base has the conventional three steps, doubled in the centre of each end for access. There was no ramp. The columns are far more slender than those at Olympia, at $5\frac{1}{2}$ times their diameter in height; but not much more slender than Aphaia, and less slender than those of their Athenian contemporary Hephaistos. Either the slightly heavier proportion was considered appropriate for a temple of this size, or the figure results from the incorporation in it of material originally prepared for the Marathon temple. The problem of the corner triglyph is here eased by adjusting the position not only of the corner column but its neighbours. The cella is abnormal, having two rooms, the larger facing east, and containing Pheidas' gold and ivory statue; the western smaller and square, perhaps used as a store room for treasure. Even with internal supporting colonnades the roof timbers reached about 12 metres, as large as was practical for the timber available at Athens. The eastern cella had two-storey Doric internal columns as at Aphaia, but with a linking section behind the statue, in front of the end wall. The western room contained four single Ionic columns, more slender than Doric and so able to reach from floor to ceiling without excessively intruding on the internal space. In front of both rooms were the porches, but unlike Aphaia, where the porches were formed by substantial extension of the side walls, with a pair of columns between, in the Parthenon the extension of the side walls was short, and the porch colonnades placed with their end columns some way in front of the side walls (in technical jargon, they are 'prostyle' rather than 'in antis'). Because of the eight column facade, the width of the cella is the equivalent of six columns which were needed, therefore, for either porch. Recent studies by Manolis Korres, the architect responsible for the current restoration and conservation of the Parthenon, have shown that there were windows high in the wall of the east porch, either side of the door into the cella – a most unusual feature in Greek temples. Both doorways were massive, and constructed in the usual Greek manner of two leaves, opening inward. They were made from specially selected cypress wood, as the building inventory tells us. All that survives of them are the marks below the threshold, the holes that once contained the metal pivots and the grooves on which they turned. Their form and appearance, like that of other wooden temple doors, can be visualised from the marble versions used in the Macedonian tombs. The door surrounds were embellished, again to the traditional Doric pattern which is found in other Doric buildings, but here in special material, attached to the marble of the walls, and now completely lost.

The Parthenon sculptures

The Parthenon was spectacular not only for its size and its use of marble. Externally, it supported more sculptured decoration than any other Greek temple. Its pediments, wider than those of Zeus, carried complex and elaborate compositions, depicting the legend of the birth of Athena at the east end, and the contest between Athena and Poseidon for the patronage of Athens on the west. On the external entablature, all ninety two metopes were decorated, with relief sculpture depicting Lapiths against Centaurs, Greeks against Trojans – combat scenes symbolising the war between Athens and Persia. As if this was not enough, the entablatures of the Doric porches were given, in place of the conventional triglyph and metope friezes, continuous Ionic-style friezes. Still further, these friezes were extended to run along the top of the walls from end to end, forming a continuous band of sculpture. The subject is a great procession, the procession of the Athenians who every four years celebrated a special festival for Athena – the Great Panathenaia. Over the centre of the east porch the frieze reaches its culmination, the handing over by Athenian maidens of the robe, the *peplos*, woven for the old traditional wooden cult statue of Athena (*not* Pheidias' new gold and ivory statue). Much of the procession, however, consists of young Athenian horsemen, representing, Sir John Boardman has suggested, the heroic dead who fell at the battle of Marathon, 192 in number. This would continue the purpose of the original temple, helping to emphasize the role of its Periklean successor as a monument celebrating the defeat of the Persians, and outdoing the temple of Zeus.

The appearance of the Parthenon

Despite the seventeenth-century explosion, much of the Parthenon survives. Most photographs show it in the form it took during the early part of the twentieth century, when it was restored by the engineer Balanos. Modern pollution, and the use by Balanos of unsuitable material has rendered this unstable, and at present a massive new programme of consolidation and repair is under way. It is useful to

Fig. 17. Side view of the Parthenon, Stillman, 1869.

compare the more ruined state of the Parthenon in the nineteenth century (though some consolidation, largely in mortared brick, can be detected), seen in figure 17, with the Balanos form, and what the Parthenon will look like when it emerges from the present restoration.

The relative completeness of the Parthenon, and the quality of its original design and construction, make it the temple in which the subtleties or refinements of the design and workmanship can be best appreciated. Although at a casual glance this, like any Greek temple, looks like a rectangular box with a lid on it, on closer study it can be seen that the box is in reality deprived of straight lines. There is a slight curvature to all three steps of the base, along the length and across the width, and this curvature is repeated in the entablature. The columns have a subtly curved profile, or entasis; in addition they are not vertical, but lean slightly inwards. This is deliberately introduced by modifying the bottom drum of each column so as to tilt it, while the tilt is 'corrected' at the capital to give a proper bearing surface to receive the entablature. The purpose of these refinements has been

Fig. 18. Three-quarter view of the Parthenon, 1975 (before the recent conservation work began).

much discussed since they were first measured and analyzed in the 1850s by F.C. Penrose. The most likely explanation is that they are for optical effect: to correct the illusion that straight and vertical lines would have induced of a building sagging at the centre and falling apart at the ends.

Another nineteenth-century discovery was that the Parthenon (like other Greek temples) was painted. There was indeed a strong reaction against the idea that such buildings could have been anything but pure white marble. In fact, in the strong Athenian sunlight newly carved and polished Pentelic marble would have been overwhelmingly dazzling. Recent study suggests that even the unpainted parts were toned down by the application of varnish. Mouldings and other parts (such as the *tainia* and *regulae* of the entablature) which require emphasis were painted in colour, vivid reds and blues and golden yellows, in the manner now known from the painted facades of the Macedonian tombs. The present appearance of Greek temples, and the black and white photographs of them, cannot do justice to their original gaudiness.

Fig. 19. Tiles of the Parthenon, reassembled by the recent conservation programme.

The temple of Hephaistos

Below the Acropolis the temple of Hephaistos is, in comparison with the Parthenon, far more conventional. It is one in a programme of temples constructed simultaneously with the Acropolis buildings and also serving as thankofferings to deities who contributed to Athens' victories over the Persians: Hephaistos the armourer, Ares of Acharnai, the god of war, Poseidon of Sounion, protector of the Athenian Fleet, and finally Nemesis of Rhamnous. 'Trade marks' in the design of all four (particularly the lining up of porch columns with the third column on the side from the end, and the extension of the porch frieze which is continuous like that of the Parthenon, not round the building but across to the back of the external frieze) demonstrate that they are either the work of one architect, or a succession of architects in a single 'school'. This temple is often called the Theseum, since its flank metopes depict the deeds of Theseus: but Theseus was a 'hero', not a god, and as such could not have a temple dedicated to him. Pausanias makes clear it is dedicated to Hephaistos, jointly with Athena, and both deities were represented in the cult statue. The temple is a more normal size, 13.708 x 31.709 m., 6 x 13 columns (of the four, only Nemesis differs significantly in dimensions, about 10 x 21.42 m., 6 x 12 columns). It is important for its excellent state of preservation, which it owes to its conversion into a church. Unlike the buildings of the Acropolis, it has not received substantial modern repairs, and its nineteenth-century appearance differs little (apart from the surroundings) from those of the present day. Compared with the Parthenon, its entablature, decorated with carved metopes at its eastern end, is relatively heavy, because the columns are more slender (5²/₃ diameter) and perhaps because it was intended particularly to be viewed from below, in the agora.

Strangely, the building seems to have taken a long time to complete: the style of the sculptural decoration suggests a date just before the outbreak of the Peloponnesian War, or even later. There are also signs of a change of plan, introduced after the original foundation had been constructed, and possibly after the erection of the external colonnade. The wall between the cella and the west (false) porch was moved slightly to the east, with more roughly constructed new foundations. Further foundations were added for an internal colonnade, modelled, it would seem, on that of the Parthenon (this was removed, along with the dividing wall, when the temple was converted into a church). The internal colonnade is unnecessary – roof timbers could easily have reached from side wall to side wall – and can only be regarded as decorative. The well-preserved upper parts of the structure give clear evidence for the form of the roof. Over the external colonnades, marble beams supporting marble ceiling slabs decorated in a coffered pattern were placed as high as possible (the rafters touch the slabs at the outer edges). Inside, the ceiling would have been wooden, with supporting beams from colonnade to colonnade. On these, centrally placed upright posts supported the sectional ridge beam; rafters ran from the cornice to a beam placed on top of the side walls, and another rafter continued the line to the ridge. Each pair of rafters supported a line of wide pantiles, each overlapping its lower successor. The joints between each row were protected by a row of ridged cover tiles, with a gutter running along the bottom (the Parthenon does not have the gutter, and the ends of its cover tiles are instead decorated with 'antefixes').

Temples similar to Hephaistos

Ares, as far as we can tell from its remains, and Poseidon were essen-

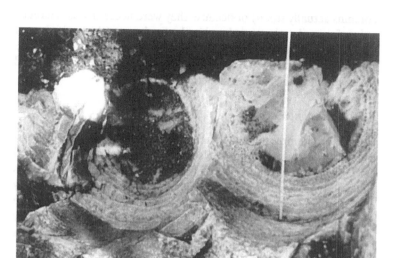

Fig. 20. Agrilesa quarries, Sounion. Holes left after cutting out drums for the columns of the temple of Poseidon.

tially similar. Poseidon was made not from Pentelic but from local (Agrilesa) marble, which was more cheaply available, despite its poorer quality. It is disfigured by veins of a dark bluish colour, and these are very noticeable in the present day, weathered state of the structure. This marble is also more friable and probably for this reason the column was given fewer, and thus shallower flutings, sixteen instead of the normal twenty. Also, most exceptionally, there is no entasis in the column shaft, either for the same reason, or as an economy. Rhamnous, too, is remote from the Pentelicus quarries, and so a conveniently local marble from Ayia Marina was used instead. This temple was left unfinished, probably because of the outbreak of the Peloponnesian War, and although badly ruined much of the superstructure survives in fragments. Originally it was structurally complete, and indeed received its cult statue, and so actually functioned as a temple; but it was never given its final polish. Projecting 'protective' surfaces are left on the stylobate surfaces, on the wall blocks, while all the columns, except those in the east porch, remained unfluted. Thus it can be seen how the builders in erecting the temple gave final treatment only to those parts where it was absolutely essential, either because some other part was to be placed on them (the sections of the stylobate, for instance, on which the columns actually stood) or because they were necessary as reference points for work to be completed in the final stage (the beginnings of the fluting can be found on the bottom column drums). This temple shows very clearly how finished Greek buildings were carved and polished out of the rougher structural body.

Later Doric temples

Later Doric temples included some large and impressive buildings, especially when these were replacements of damaged or destroyed earlier structures. The temple of Apollo at Delphi, and that of Zeus at Nemea (the sanctuary where the Nemean games were traditionally celebrated) were both rebuilt in the fourth century, on the foundations and essentially to the same plan as their sixth-century predecessors. The temple of Athena Alea at Tegea in Arcadia is another substantial fourth-century replacement for an earlier predecessor, famous for its decorative sculpture which was the work of Scopas, one of the leading fourth-century sculptors. 'New' temples, which do not replace earlier predecessors, may be represented by the temple of Asklepios at Epidauros. This is important more for the evidence from its related building inscriptions than its actual remains, being very badly ruined. It was well built, from good Corinthian limestone rather than marble, and decorated with sculpture. But it is on a small scale, 11.75 m. x 23.06 m., and though peripteral had only 6 x 11 columns. Epidauros in the fourth century, and the cult of Asklepios, although aspiring to international significance did not command the resources available to Athens in the preceding century. Even so, this temple was decorated with a structurally unnecessary internal colonnade. No evidence for its form survives, but it is probable that like other later temples at Epidauros, and the temples at Nemea and Tegea, the internal columns were in the newly developing Corinthian order. A solitary example of a Corinthian column occurs in the otherwise Ionic interior of the temple of Apollo at Bassae, a temple attributed by Pausanias to Iktinos – an attribution universally rejected as improbable by modern scholars.

Few Doric temples can be dated to the Hellenistic age. Greece was well endowed with buildings of earlier date, which were generally kept in repair. But the financial decay of mainland Greece was not conducive to new building. The Macedonians had adopted the Doric tradition and exported it through Alexander's conquests. There were Doric temples at Alexandria, and in Syria, though little good evidence survives. Best preserved and understood is the temple of Athena Polias at Pergamon. It was built towards the middle of the third century BC by the Attalid rulers of Pergamon, desiring to stress either their (probably pseudo) Macedonian connections, or the definitely fictitious legendary foundation of their city by Dorian Argos. This temple commits the solecism of spacing the columns so widely that three, rather than two, sets of triglyphs and metopes were needed for each pair of columns.

Ionic temples

It was not, therefore, surprising that in the second century the Ionic architect Hermogenes, called on by the King of Pergamon to build a Doric temple to Dionysus, refused and insisted instead on reasserting the local tradition of the East Greek cities – to build in Ionic. The Ionic order had not experienced the same quantity of temple building in the fifth century that we see in the Doric area of the mainland. The Ionian cities were subject to Athens, and their surplus funds were diverted as tribute. Indeed, it was Athens as the mother city of the Ionians who built Ionic temples in the fifth century: the replacement for the 'old' temple on the Acropolis (see below, Chapter 5), the little temple of Nike at the entrance to the Acropolis (where the Doric order would be too clumsy for the scale of the building), and the temple of Artemis Agrotera by the river Ilissus. It was only during the political and economic revival of the East Greek cities in the later fourth century, particularly after their liberation by Alexander the Great, that important new Ionic temples were constructed there. Work started on rebuilding the colossal sixth-century temple of Artemis at Ephesus on the original foundations, immediately after its destruction by fire in 356. The earlier temple measured 55.10 m. x 115.14 m., with two rows of columns (8 x 21 externally) all round. The centre spacing of the facade was wider than the others, and at 8.62 m. give the largest architrave blocks known in Greek architecture. It was built of marble. The cella was too wide to be spanned by single beams, yet no traces of an inner colonnade have been found. Probably it was unroofed. The temple was set on low-lying ground, and liable to flooding. The later version was given a higher platform to avoid this, but was otherwise similar – apart from an additional row of columns for its façade.

Temple of Athena at Priene

There are two more original Ionic temples. That of Athena Polias at Priene was the work of Pytheos, one of the architects who worked on the Mausoleum. It is a modest structure compared with Ephesus, 19.53 x 37.13 m. with 6 x 13 columns. The cella wall is placed close to the colonnade, which has a ceiling of single coffer slabs with sculptured decoration – an arrangement previously used by Pytheos on the Mausoleum. There is a shallow false porch at the back of the cella, unusual for Ionic temples and perhaps indicating mainland Doric influence. The form of the Ionic order, though, is traditional. The columns have bases decorated in the conventional eastern or Asiatic manner and the entablature has a dentil, but no continuous sculptured frieze. The temple was sufficiently complete for it to be dedicated by Alexander when he passed Priene in his invasion of the Persian empire in 334 BC.

Hermogenes' masterpiece

The other temple is later, probably mid-second century, and is Hermogenes' masterpiece, dedicated to Artemis at Magnesia on the Maeander. This, too, replaces a sixth-century predecessor, of which little is known; and we cannot tell if it influenced Hermogenes' replacement or not. It is interesting for two things. In it, Hermogenes revives the pseudo-dipteral form, where there is space for a double external colonnade; but only the outer row of columns is actually built. The Roman architect and engineer Vitruvius, who derives his knowledge of Ionic form, and the complex theories of design, proportion and column spacing from now lost handbooks written by Hermogenes, credits him with the invention of this system. It is more likely, however, that he is reviving something that was already known in the sixth century. The other interesting feature is that here, at last, we have an example of the final, standardized form of Ionic, which is inherited by the Romans. The columns even here in Eastern Greece (and unlike the earlier temple of Artemis at Magnesia) have the Athenian rather than the Asiatic type of base; and the entablature has, over a double moulding that is one of Hermogenes' trademarks, a continuous sculptured frieze, rather jejeunely carved, combined with a dentil frieze. The Greek geographer Strabo, rather surprisingly, says this is the most beautiful of Ionic temples, though it would have been impressive enough. It comes from the end of the

Hellenistic period. Already Greek architects were experimenting with Corinthian temples (Zeus at Athens, Zeus at Olba in Cilicia), and it is with this order, rather, that the Roman future lies.

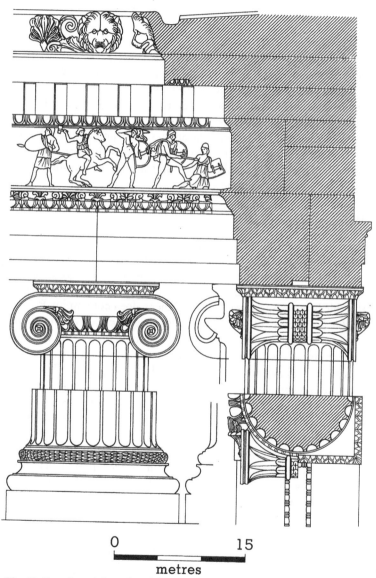

0   15
metres

Fig. 21. Drawing of the order of the temple of Artemis, Magnesia.

Chapter 4
Other Types of Building

Only gradually did Greek cities acquire a whole range of non-religious, or ancillary buildings which can be regarded as true architecture. Even so, when these other buildings are constructed, although they may vary considerably in function and so in form from the temple, the architectural principles and methods which were evolved for temples were used. This means that they are in a sense dependent on temple architecture, and can only be fully understood as part of one and the same system.

The question of expense

There is a wide range of materials used in them, depending on cost and availability. Since the expenses of building include transport of materials as well as the processes of construction, if good quality material is available locally, it is often no more expensive than poorer. But this is most infrequent. Even Athens does not employ Pentelic marble for its more utilitarian buildings. The limestone of Piraeus was of good quality, and more accessible; for this reason it was used extensively. A second expense is the preparation of stone, shaping it to a precise dimension and fitting the blocks together. The softer forms of limestone (*poros* stone) are more easily worked: less man hours are required for their preparation, and so money is saved, and also less accurate work can be tolerated. Quite respectable buildings can be constructed of *poros*, and if a superior finish is required, just as in those temples which were forced to use inferior stone, this can be achieved by the addition of a stucco finish. Cheapest of all is brick: unbaked mudbrick, since the general shortage of wood in Greece makes the firing of kilns for terracotta expensive, and this material was only used where durability was necessary, for tiles and other (often decorative) coverings. Thirdly, the roofing timbers. The large timbers needed for temples like the Parthenon, and even the more modest beams employed in temples of more normal size, such as those of Hephaistos, had to be imported and were very expensive. The restrictions of size for other buildings were therefore more severe.

Public buildings with large roof spans invariably involved expense. Thus the development of public, as opposed to religious, architecture was slower. It is only after the conquests of Alexander released the resources of the Persian Empire that the Greek cities begin to put up buildings other than temples on a substantial scale. Even then, it is noticeable that many cities relied on gifts from the Hellenistic kings to pay for such structures, and those communities which were not able to attract royal munificence generally continued to be architecturally impoverished.

Colonnades and courtyards

Two architectural arrangements dominate these buildings: the extended colonnades, and the courtyard. The colonnade derives directly from the embellishment of temples, but is put to a utilitarian function. The extended colonnade was a cheap and effective way of providing shade and shelter. The resulting structure is called a stoa, and this becomes an essential and widespread feature of Greek architecture. At its simplest, it consists of a single step acting as a support for the line of posts, which may be wooden rather than stone columns. Behind this, the floor is of beaten earth, rather than the careful and expensive paving of temple floors. The roof slopes down from the rear wall to the entablature (wood, if the posts are wooden) of the facade. An extra internal line of posts makes possible a ridged roof, like that of a temple, but the woodwork of the roof was normally visible from inside and not concealed behind a ceiling, as in a temple.

Such colonnades generally formed a boundary to an open space. By the seventh century Greek houses had developed from simple huts to more complex plans, of rooms round a central (or even off-centre) courtyard. Such a system is sensible in the context both of the Greek climate and the development of Greek social attitudes. The courtyard provided reasonable light, but at the same time made shading of rooms possible. It allowed easy ventilation in the hot summer, and protection from the poorer weather of winter. Above all, it afforded privacy to societies which tended to insist on the segregation and seclusion of women. The concept of enclosed space, for shelter and privacy, differs from that of the temple – the building isolated in open space – but is equally, if not more, important for the development of Greek architecture.

The agora

All this can be seen in the treatment of the agora. As a technical term, this cannot be translated into English, since English towns do not function in the same way as Greek cities. The word means, essentially, the place where people gather, an open space where the citizens – the men – can come together, possibly for buying and selling, but more often for political and judical purposes, and to administer the community of which they were part. All that was needed for this was an open field (and this, for example, is where the citizens of Sparta gather when summoned by their kings). As Greek cities became socially and administratively more complex, the need to set aside an area within the built-up limits of the city became stronger, and its various functions tended to require buildings to house them.

Stoas

Even when the agora was architecturally fully developed, the concept of it as an open space remained. Its buildings were therefore concentrated on its perimeter and it became, in effect, a large courtyard. It was to achieve this that the stoa came into its own. Colonnades erected along the edge of the agora helped to define it,

Fig. 22. Stoa in sanctuary of Artemis, Brauron.

and give it a sense of unity. They could also be adapted to a variety of purposes; and it is clear that the stoa should be regarded as a general type, rather than a specific building with a defined function. It is impossible, briefly, to categorize all the different variants of stoa form. Instead, the stoa should be regarded as a building which can be adapted to meet different circumstances which create variable arrangments. The simplest are straight colonnades, as long as are necessary, or to fill the available space; but the colonnades can turn corners, so that a stoa can be two or three-sided, or even join up round all sides of a rectangle to form a completely enclosing portico. It is usually an economy to add an internal colonnade, and so double the available roofed space. Triple colonnades are not unknown, but much rarer, and there are examples of multiple systems. Stoas can act as the facades to rooms, or series of rooms which are their functional heart: these can be shops, dining rooms, law courts, archive rooms, administrative offices. Each example has to be interpreted in its own context.

In the fifth century some stoas, particularly those at Athens, were quite substantial buildings and of architectural merit. They were almost always built with Doric columns: Doric columns and capitals were easier to carve than Ionic, and thus cheaper. For this reason, when in the Hellenistic period the East Greek cities built a very large

Fig. 23. Interior view of north Stoa, agora of Priene.

number of stoas, despite the local Ionic tradition, Doric was invariably used (one feels that Hermogenes, in rejecting the Doric order as unsuitable for temples, regarded it as best used for these lesser buildings, particularly as the corner triglyph problem was less obvious in an extended colonnade). Further economy could be achieved by spacing the columns more widely than in temples, with three sets of triglyphs and metopes to each pair of columns, rather than two. For these colonnades, anything more than a single step would have been too ponderous. Internal columns which supported the ridge beam directly, rather than horizontal ceiling beams, needed to be taller than the outer colonnades, and so were generally Ionic. Since they carried a wooden beam and not a stone entablature, they could be spaced more widely than the outer columns, generally at double the interval. Two-storey stoas are even more economical of ground space, but are quite late in developing: the earliest seem to have been built at about 300 BC. Multi-storey stoas are a particular feature of Hellenistic architecture at Pergamon and its dependencies (and were 'exported' as gifts to cities which the Pergamene kings wished to favour. Athens was given one for the redevelopment of its agora by the second-century BC King Attalus II). They are often used on steeply sloping sites (such as the acropolis of Pergamon itself) partly as outward facing facades in front of terrace walls used to level up platforms, while their upper storeys face inward to the platform.

Council buildings

There are other categories of public building associated with the agora. In later times, the Cleisthenic Council, and similar councils in other cities, met in closed buildings. These were rectangular or square, with high side walls and windows placed high in them, well above the level at which it would have been possible to see in. Inside, seats were arranged either along three sides of the wall, or as a semicircle (the first Council house at Athens, perhaps dating to the 470s, was of the first type; it was replaced at the end of the fifth century by a new building, of the second type). If the Council house was square, it might have a pyramidal roof rising to a central point; otherwise, the conventional ridge and gable type was employed. The architectural problem was to roof sufficient space to accommodate a Council of 500 (as at Athens) without obstructive internal supports. Council houses, therefore, often had roof beams as large as any in the largest Greek temples.

Fig. 24. Assembly (? Council) building, Priene.

Structures to accommodate larger numbers than the 500 or so of Council buildings emphasize the weak points of Greek architectural technique. Large gatherings were not unusual in Classical Greece: meetings of the democratic assemblies numbered thousands, as did the audiences at the dramatic festivals or the spectators at athletic contests. Only rarely did such gatherings take place in closed buildings, under roofs. There is an assembly building at Megalopolis in Arcadia, and a building at Athens called an *odeion*, or 'music hall', built under the auspices of Perikles. They both demonstrate the same architectural weakness, having high pyramidal roofs which were supported on a veritable forest of posts – those of the *odeion* of Perikles supposedly made from the masts of Xerxes' warships, abandoned after the battle of Salamis. It takes the different roofing technologies available to Roman architects to develop the Basilica, which is one solution to this architectural problem.

Theatres

Where secrecy was not a requirement, buildings for large gatherings in the Greek world were open air. Dramatic and athletic contests were watched by spectators seated on the natural slopes of a hillside, which thus determined the position where they were held. Any architectural

Fig. 25. Theatre of Dionysus, Athens (J. Pascal Sebah, 1870s).

enhancement of this was slight before the fifth century BC, though by that time wooden seating was provided for audiences in the Theatre of Dionysus at Athens. Stone was an alternative material, used in one or two small rural theatres such as that at Thorikos in Eastern Attica. The fully developed Classical theatres, such as the splendidly presented example at Epidauros, are essentially the product of the fourth century or later. The central feature was the circular dancing floor (the *orchestra*) for the choral dancing from which drama developed. This can be seen in all Greek theatres, even in the Hellenistic age when the dramatic role of the chorus was no longer required except for the 'revivals' of fifth-century plays. Behind the *orchestra* came the stage and stage buildings, temporary and wooden in the fifth century, but of stone in the Hellenistic age and with a high raised stage, such as that in the second-century BC theatre of Priene. The audience sits on stone seats invariably extended round the *orchestra* for a little more than the semicircle. They are divided into wedge-shaped blocks by access stairways running up from the level of the *orchestra*, and often also into lower and upper sections by an

Fig. 26. Theatre at sanctuary of Asklepios, Epidauros.

intervening walkway (the largest theatres, such as that at Pergamon, have three sections). Most seats are placed on a natural hillside, and so theatres are generally located where a hollow hillside of the required profile is available. But, probably beginning with Athens in the fifth century, the natural slopes are modified by constructing support walls (*parodos* walls) at the planned ends of the seating, and filling up the space behind them with terracing to support the seats. Theatres might also be used for political meeting places, or a special meeting place not unlike a theatre might be provided such as the Pnyx at Athens.

Stadiums

The stadiums for athletic contests develop in the same way. At first, these are completely natural running courses, perhaps in slight valleys with sloping sides on which the spectators sit. These are enhanced by artificial terracing and stone seats, until they display the familiar long narrow form. The curved end to the stadium is found at least as early as that built for the Nemean games around 325 BC, but early Greek stadiums are often straight ended.

Fig. 27. The Stadium, Epidauros.

The courtyard

Other athletic activities – exercise and gymnastics, in particular – take up the idea of the enclosed colonnaded courtyard. Here, again, in the fifth century no architectural embellishment was required: the gymnasium, such as the Academy at Athens – is simply an open space, the only shade being provided by trees. In the Hellenistic cities the gymnasia develop as schools (philosophical schools at Athens are exceptions), the place for the general education of the young male citizens. Here the closed courtyard principle gives the seclusion and privacy required, with rooms opening off the courtyard for classes. Gymnasia are found in both cities and sanctuaries and are an essential indication of prosperity in the Hellenistic age.

The Greek house

Above all, the courtyard is the principle on which the Classical Greek house is based. The developed form of Greek housing is, in essentials, universal in the cities, probably by the sixth century BC. Simple huts are found in Dark Age levels, and a whole town of them exists, dating to the eighth/seventh century BC at the modern Emporio on the south coast of Chios. The Greek colonies of the west, such as Himera, have full courtyard plans in the sixth century, and the increasing evidence from fifth-century Athens suggests it was the normal type there. These houses are not public architecture, and they are built, generally, from the resources of individual families. It is here we see the intuitive and traditional methods of vernacular architecture, modified perhaps by changing social and historical circumstances, but evolving slowly. Even in fifth-century Athens, walls are invariably of mudbrick (so that the Greek word for a housebreaker means literally a 'wall digger', a man who enters a house by digging a hole through its mudbrick wall). Tiled roofs are normal, at least on the mainland, but the plans are very often irregular, and the roof line varied. Many houses were of single storey type only, but the evidence for staircases – or at least steps – shows that upper floors were common.

The courtyard gave access to the different rooms placed around it: the entrance to it was usually off-centre, and, to increase privacy, normally situated so that no direct view of the interior was possible. There were colonnades inside the more sumptuous houses, and in the most extravagant these may have been of stone. So we are approaching a context in which the house is becoming part of architecture; but until the Hellenistic age stone colonnades must have been very rare – no certain examples are known – and wooden posts were usual. Such lines of posts were generally restricted to one side of the court, supporting either a sloping roof or, in two storey buildings, a balcony giving access to the rooms of an upper floor. Courtyards with posts and roofs round all four sides – full peristyle courts – were rare in the Classical period, though examples are found at Olynthus. They are much more common in the sumptuous houses of the Hellenistic age such as those at Pella, the capital of Macedonia.

There are also examples of 'official' houses, places designated as the residences of state officials during their period of office, or providing for official activities some of the functions of a house. Many Greek houses (very noticeably those at Olynthus) had special rooms for all-male feasting and drinking parties. Such a room is called the *andron*, and is the setting, for example, of the gathering described in Plato's Symposium. In these, the participants reclined on couches placed round the walls of the room, rather than sat to table; low tables in front of each couch carried the food. Feasting could be both private, in the private houses, and public, on state or religious

Fig. 28. Black-figure cup showing diners on a couch, University of Birmingham. Photograph by Graham Norrie.

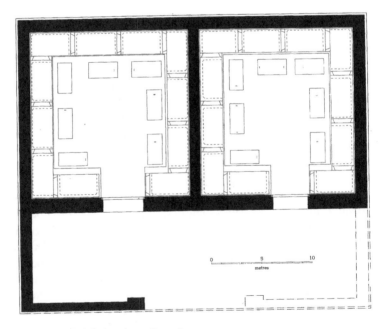

Fig. 29. Plan of dining room, Perachora.

occasions, so dining rooms are found in public buildings as well as sanctuaries. They can usually be recognized by raised plinths round the walls on which the couches were placed; by the off-centre position of the entrance door, necessitated by the way the couches were arranged; and on occasion, by evidence for the couches themselves, which in some sanctuaries were carved from blocks of stone. It is for these reasons that we know that some, at least, of the rooms behind the late fifth-century stoa on the south side of the Athenian agora were dining rooms. Dining rooms were measured by the number of couches which could be placed round their walls; those of the agora south stoa were seven-couch rooms. Such rooms are also attached to courtyard buildings, opening off the surrounding courtyard. A good example is that built at Athens, again at the end of the fifth century or early in the fourth, as the place where the procession of the Panathenaic festival could be marshalled, the *Pompeion* (presumably the procession had always gathered in this locality, but it had not been thought necessary to provide a building for it). It is an interesting example of the practice of economy in the construction of non-essential public buildings. Apart from the flourish of a marble entrance porch, the walls were of unbaked mudbrick, the columns plain shafts on disc bases, the entablature made of wood. Projecting beyond the courtyard wall into the irregularly shaped space available between it and the city walls were six dining rooms, two seven-couch rooms, two eleven-couch rooms, two fifteen-couch rooms.

These various buildings have in common an architectural tradition, in terms of material, technique, and design, which gave an essential unity to the Greek cities. The strength of this unity can be seen in the failure, largely, of Greek architects to exploit the invention of the stone barrel vault, developed for the tombs of the Macedonian kings at Aegeae about the middle of the fourth century BC. The advantage of such roofs for tombs buried underground is that, unlike the wooden roofs of most Greek buildings, they do not decay. It is this fact that has preserved for us intact the vaulted tomb of Philip II, built for his assassinated father by Alexander the Great, and still containing when it was discovered by Professor Andronikos in 1978 the rich offerings buried with him. These semicircular roofs do not agree with the angular forms of normal, timber-supported ridge and pediment roofs; and the thrust of the stone vaulting against the side walls requires special support, easy for buried tombs, less easy for other buildings. But monumental tombs are not a feature of normal Greek architecture. The most splendid, the original Mausoleum at Halicarnassus, was built by Greek architects for a Carian, non-Greek dynast; and even Philip's position as king of Macedonia is part of a political system alien to that of the Greek city states. Vaults find a use over gateways in fortifications, where they are supported by the curtain walls to either side; and over entrance passages, buried in earth like the Macedonian tombs that lead into the Stadium at Nemea and the auditorium of the theatre at Sikyon – both buildings which were almost certainly put up by Kings of Macedonian origin.

Chapter 5

Buildings in their Context – Sanctuaries

Worship of the god

Greek temples did not function in the same way as churches. They were not buildings intended to hold congregations at religious services, but instead provided shelter for the statue of the god or image and the more valuable offerings made to him – those which needed to be kept under lock and key. Accessibility to the interior of the temple was restricted. Worship took the form of festivals, which were generally annual (though there might well be other occasions for corporate worship in the religious calendar). For important cults and divinities the festival was open to all, even slaves. Very large numbers of worshippers would participate, and no closed building could accommodate them. The central act was the offering of sacrifices, at an altar in the open air, in the presence of the multitude of worshippers. The sacrifice was burnt on the altar, so that the smoke and the smell would drift up to the sky, to the abode of the god on Mt Olympus. At the same time the image of the god also watched, from the temple, the performance of the ritual. Thus the place of worship was the whole sanctuary, rather than specifically the temple building in it, and the focus was the open air altar. The first requirement, therefore, for the practice of Greek religion was an area set aside for the worship of the god. The area so dedicated depended on the importance of the deity, and the number of worshippers the festival was likely to attract. Each Greek city had its own patron deity, and for this deity a major sanctuary would be necessary. Other deities might protect smaller sections of the community. Most Greek cities, in fact, contained a surprising number of very small sanctuaries that served these more restricted cults.

The site for a sanctuary

The reasons for the choice of particular spots to serve as sanctuaries must have been varied, and are usually unknown, though we may deduce them. The choice of the Acropolis at Athens as the sanctuary of Athena derives from its central place in Athenian history. It was the heart of the city. It had served as the fortified stronghold and palace of the Mycenaean rulers of Athens, and its massive walls survived into the historical period. Just as the kings had been the protectors of the city, so was Athena. It was here that she contested with Poseidon for the patronage of Athens. In the Classical period the Athenians could see the signs of that struggle, the salt 'sea', or pool, where Poseidon struck the Acropolis rock with his trident, and the sacred olive tree which was Athena's winning gift to them. A tradition of importance – and probably sanctity – running continuously from the Bronze Age was thus explained and rationalised.

But this is only putting back the selection of the site to an earlier date. Natural phenomena may explain the choice. A particularly abundant spring, important in the hot dry summers of Greece, is an adequate reason, and certainly helps explain the religious significance of Delphi. So is the physical appearance of the surrounding countryside. The power of religious usage can be demonstrated by those Greek cities whose major sanctuaries are not situated within the limits of the town, but at some distance. The major sanctuary of Argos, the Argive Heraion, is on the opposite side of the Argive plan to the Classical city, on a site which had been significant in the Bronze Age when the political geography of the Argolid was different.

The first requirement for a sanctuary is space. The next requirement is demarcation – the creation of a boundary separating the area of the god from the secular world; but even this need not be a wall, so long as it was clearly defined. Subsequently, the provision of accommodation became necessary. The cult image needed to be housed. A small shrine building would be adequate, though for reasons of prestige and piety they develop into fully fledged temples. In theory, it is likely that other activities which we know take place in the sanctuaries go back to early origins, but the evidence is non-existent.

Processions are always an important part of Greek religion – the Athenian procession to the Acropolis at the Panathenaic festival of Athena, the procession from Athens to Eleusis for the celebration of the mysteries of Demeter and Kore. Similarly with the contests, both athletic and artistic. The Greeks believed that the Olympic games were first held in the year we would call 776 BC, but they have not left any trace of that date in the archaeological record of Olympia. Buildings are, above all, embellishment; and it is the desire to achieve this which is the driving force in the architectural development of the sanctuaries. They are to be regarded, like the gold and silver cups, the bronzes, the statues, the humble terracotta figures, and the pots which are deposited in the sanctuaries, as offerings to the gods, intended to impress them and to secure their support for the mortals who are their dependants, and whose festivals acknowledge their dependency.

The Acropolis of Athens

No single period, or century, typifies, and it is necessary in order to understand each sanctuary, to try to trace its development. The Acropolis of Athens retained throughout the Dark Age and into the Classical period the visible evidence that in the Late Bronze Age it had been a fortified stronghold. It was only with the development of the Classical city below its slopes that its military function waned, though it was still defended against Xerxes in 480 BC. The earliest surviving real evidence for its use as a sanctuary is probably the story of the would-be tyrant, Kylon, and his supporters seeking refuge at the altar of Athena after the failure of his coup towards the end of the seventh century BC. But clearly the sanctuary had been in existence for centuries before that. The sacred area was delineated by the Mycenaean fortification wall, and at this date the entrance to it must have been through a massive gateway, probably similar in arrangement to the 'Lion Gate' at Mycenae. There are no real traces of the altar to Athena, which was at the highest point in front of the surviving remains of the earliest 'old temple'. These are foundations of roughly shaped but worked blocks for a cella, with rooms facing east and west, fronted by porches and surrounded by a peripteral colonnade. In its final form, the colonnade comprised 6 x 12 Doric columns. The pediments included sculptured groups, part of which, a central figure of Athena in combat with a giant, is preserved in the Acropolis Museum. The style of this demonstrates that it was put up around 525 BC; it was destroyed by the Persians, and a stretch of its entablature was then rebuilt into the new north wall of the Acropolis – presumably as a memorial. But the origin of the temple is much earlier than this. The outer foundation shows traces of the use of a claw chisel, and this suggests that it is not original. It may have been added for the final temple (this is the date when the claw chisel was first used at Delphi) but it probably belongs to an earlier reconstruction when the building was given pediment decoration (which included the triple headed 'Bluebeard' figure, again preserved in the

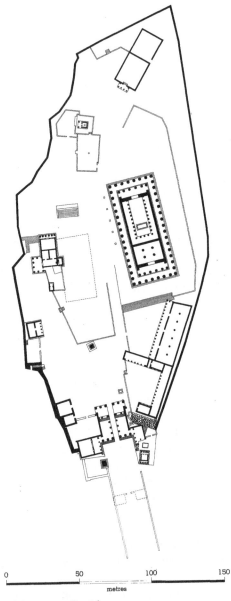

Fig. 30. Plan of the Acropolis, Athens.

Acropolis Museum). What existed before this is less certain but, apart from the use of the claw chisel, there is no reason why the peripteral form – perhaps with wooden columns – should not date back to the seventh century. An even earlier, but simpler shrine building on this site is a logical certainty. This was the building which housed the venerable statue of Athena, carved in olive wood and clothed in the real robe, the *peplos*, which was woven for it by young Athenian maidens. This statue was evacuated with the Athenians to Salamis when Xerxes invaded, and so survived the destruction of the Acropolis.

To the north of the temple was the precinct of the nymph Pandrosos; by this was the sacred olive tree of Athena, and a little to one side, the salt 'sea' of Poseidon. The tomb of Kekrops, the early king of Athens, was by the northern foundation wall of the temple. In this vicinity, too, were the mysterious steps at the bottom of which priestesses as part of the annual ritual had to place a bundle, which then disappeared. (Excavation in the 1930s revealed that these steps were all that was left of a well which had been constructed to supply the Acropolis with an emergency water supply during the thirteenth century BC, and which had long since gone out of use.)

Much impetus was given by the development of the Panathenaic festival – particularly the 'Great' Panathenaia, celebrated every four years like the major festivals of the Olympic Games, and instituted in 566 BC by Hippokleides. From this date we can be certain that the festival included the Panathenaic procession. Perhaps the penultimate rebuilding of the temple was part of this development.

Eventually the decision was taken to complete the effective demilitarization of the Acropolis, by dismantling the old gateway and building instead a decorative propylon. This had a Doric facade to front and back, and a wall for doors, including a central door through which the procession would pass, and which was probably opened only for the procession. This new propylon was not complete when it had to be defended against Xerxes, and was damaged by fire.

The Acropolis destroyed

The Persians completely ruined the Acropolis. They destroyed the temple of Athena and smashed all the marble statues which stood around it, depicting the young maidens who had served Athena as priestesses (the '*korai*'), and the other monuments. They destroyed also the scaffolding and all that had been erected of a great new temple, situated to the south of the traditional temple, of Pentelic marble and constituting a thank offering to Athena for the victory over the Persians at Marathon in 490, the predecessor of the Parthenon. After the Persians were driven out, the Acropolis was tidied up, but not rebuilt. The propylon was patched with secondhand material, but the Parthenon building was abandoned – the cella, or perhaps only the west cella, of the old temple turned into a storehouse for the treasures dedicated to Athena. Her cult statue was brought back from Salamis and housed in a temporary structure to the north of the old temple. The failure to rebuild is noticeable, and can only be explained by a religious taboo – a vow to leave the destruction in perpetuity as a memorial to Persian sacrilege. By the middle of the century this was no longer acceptable. Either a deliberate decision was taken to release the city from the vow, or else it was interpreted rather as a vow not to rebuild until the Persians were finally defeated, and it was now judged this moment had come.

The rebuilding of the Acropolis

The new plan involved some alteration of the arrangements on the Acropolis, but is essentially based on the earlier building to commemorate Marathon which had been thwarted by Xerxes. Work was restarted in 447 on the colossal Doric temple on the south side, the Parthenon, to the new design of Iktinos and Kallikrates (see Chapter 3 above). It was structurally complete and dedicated at the Panathenaic festival of 438, though work continued on the sculptural decoration until 433. Visually, this great temple dominated the Acropolis, and would have dwarfed the old temple, if this had been rebuilt on the old foundations. Instead, the decision was taken to demolish what was left of the old temple, and to create a new temple to the north (generally called the Erechtheion). The outbreak of the Peloponnesian war interrupted this: the new temple was not started until after the peace of Nikias and, after an interruption and an accidental fire, only completed in 406 BC. It was designed to be in the Ionic rather than the Doric order. By this time the political distinction between the Dorian allies of Sparta and the Ionians of the Athenian empire was clear. Athens claimed to be the mother city of the Ionians and the choice of Ionic for the new temple emphasized the political circumstances.

The Erechtheion

The position of the Erechtheion is at the edge of the Acropolis rock, which is here lower than where the old temple had stood. It would have been simple, as with the Parthenon, to build a deep foundation to support the new building and to level up the site with terracing; but this would have buried the salt 'sea' of Poseidon, the tomb of Kekrops and the other sacred spots which marked this area. Instead, the new building was deliberately designed to incorporate them undisturbed and to act as an architectural embellishment of them. The result is like no other Greek temple. It is built on two levels, the higher to the east, the lower to the west and north. Like the old temple it has a double cella: one facing east, with the cult statue, and at the higher level; the other to the west, divided like its predecessor into anteroom and two inner chambers, at the lower level. The west wall comes over the tomb of Kekrops, which was not disturbed; there are no foundations here, and the tomb was bridged by a single massive block of marble suspended under the corner of the cella building – a structural weakness. There were six Ionic columns at the east end. The cella building has a single roof level, and columns at the west end would have been out of scale if they had had to reach from the ground to the level of the entablature which had been determined by the

Fig. 31. The Erechtheion (from the west, before recent conservation work).

eastern colonnade. They therefore are placed, as half columns between antae rather than a full colonnade, on the west wall, their bases at the same level as those of their eastern counterparts. Much more eccentric are two additional porches on the sides at the west end. That which projects south, towards the centre of the Acropolis, is small. Instead of Ionic columns, it is supported by statues of maidens (the *Korai* – they are frequently called the Karyatids but this is not the proper term for them), derived from similar supports in sixth century buildings at Delphi; (the Treasury of Siphnos – see below) but surely recalling the sixth-century dedicatory statues which had once stood in this area, and whose broken remains had been buried in the vicinity. The porch on the opposite, north side is larger, and employs Ionic columns which are bigger than those of the east porch but, being set at the lower ground level, are still not tall enough to bring their entablature to the level of that on the main cella building. Most curious is a hole deliberately left in the porch roof, directly above the salt 'sea' of Poseidon – presumably so that if Poseidon wanted to repeat his action in striking the Acropolis with his trident, the blow would not damage the building. The porch appears to be partly the embellishment of these features; but it is also the principal entrance to the west cella, through a large and lavishly decorated door opening. It is not aligned with the end of the temple, but projects to the west; in the projection is another doorway, the entrance to the Pandrosos precinct. Other architectural abnormalities include large windows to either side of the door at the east end, far more prominent than those now known to have existed at the east end of the Parthenon; and the continuous friezes of the Ionic entablatures made from dark grey Eleusinian limestone, with carved figures attached to it in Pentelic marble.

Thus the plan of the Erechtheion is complicated. But it is clear from the way the different parts are placed against each other that the architect had difficulty visualizing it as an organic entity: he thought in terms of separate boxes, even allowing detail to be carved on the main cella block which was to be totally covered by the construction of the adjacent north porch. This demonstrates that no proper drawn out scale plan or elevation of the building was prepared before the construction was carried out. It also shows the difficulties Greek architects experienced if they ventured away from the simple straightforward and conventional forms that already existed.

The Propylaia

Fig. 32. The Propylaia, from inside the Acropolis (Stillman, 1869). The defensive needs for the entrance at this end were reemphasised when the Propylaia was converted into a medieval castle. Of this the curtain walls (not visible in this photograph) still survived in 1869 as well as the Frankish tower which stands in this photo on the south-west wing of Propylaia. It was demolished, at the expense of Heinrich Schliemann, six years after this photo was taken, to reveal the Classical structure it incorporated.

The same problems had already occurred in the new version of the gateway building, the Propylaia. The architect was Mnesikles, and he was justly famed for the splendour and success of his achievement. It was started in 436, after the conclusion of work on the Parthenon, and was left unfinished at the outbreak of the Peloponnesian war. The axis of the building was moved into alignment with the length of the Acropolis, and at the head of its continuation, in the form of a steep ramp, along the line of approach. At the top of the ramp were four steps, broken at the centre by the continuation of the ramp through the building as a passageway for the sacred procession and sacrificial

Fig. 33. A modern view of the Propylaia, for comparison. Note where ancient blocks have been restored to their original position and form. New conservation work is in progress.

animals. The steps continued forward at either side, but here they were at the top of a support wall, marked off by a course of Eleusinian limestone, and inaccessible. The main facade was like a temple, six Doric columns with a pediment over. Behind was a deep porch, a row of Ionic columns either side of the passageway supporting the ceiling and roof. At the back was a second flight of steps below the cross wall which had five doors, a large ceremonial door at the centre for the procession, two lesser doors to either side, the outer ones smaller than the inner pair. Behind this wall, at a higher level (and so with a higher roof) was a shallow porch of six columns placed on a single step. These columns were of the same proportions as those of the Parthenon, with which they provided a visual link; the outer columns were slightly more slender. The platform of the outer porch continues above the steps to right and left of the ramp; and on this, above the steps, were placed smaller Doric facades – three columns between antae, projecting from walls running out to north and south from the main porch building. Viewed from below, from the ramp, these give the effect of balance and symmetry; and this is the cleverness of the design, since the buildings behind them are not identical.

Pinakotheke and temple of Nike

To the north is a square room, its porch wall having an off-centre door with windows to either side. Pausanias tells us it was a picture gallery – the *Pinakotheke*. The presence of paintings suggest, and the off-centre door really proves, that this was a formal dining room where important people could consume the meat from the sacrifice. The south wing of the Propylaia had a blank wall, where the north had the wall with doors and windows. In front of this was a bench for offerings, recalling one which had existed in roughly the same position by the earlier propylon (and in fact antedating it); so probably the dining room *Pinakotheke* also replaces an earlier, independent building. The south wing instead leads on to the projecting bastion, part of the old Mycenaean fortifications but now recased in regular masonry. On this was the separate sanctuary of Athena Nike, where, subsequently, during the peace of Nicias a small Ionic temple was erected. Definitely planned, but never executed, were further rooms, one behind the north and one behind the south wing (the side walls of the main porch show where the roofs and ridge beams of these rooms were to run into them). They would have helped to create, with their intermediate roof levels, a better link between the outer wings and the main structure; but they are not structurally necessary. This is by far the most impressive entrance building, even in its incomplete form, to any Greek sanctuary.

Architectural development of the Acropolis

Other buildings on the Acropolis are, visually, less important. To the right of the Propylaia, just inside the Acropolis is the precinct of Brauronian Artemis, whose main cult centre is in eastern Attica. This precinct marks the assimilation of her cult into the main Athenian Pantheon. Between this and the Parthenon was the armoury (*Chalkotheke*) where the suits of hoplite armour dedicated to Athena at the Great Panathenaic festival were stored.

Judged only from the buildings, there appears to have been much empty space on the Acropolis, but in the Classical period this was covered with statues and other dedications. There were innumerable special sacred places; and a particular sanctity attached to the buildings: the steps of the Parthenon, particularly at the west end, were a favourable place for dedications, and the slots into which they were fitted can still be seen. It is difficult to visualise the chaotic arrangement, punctuated only by the now carefully placed buildings and the processional routes which led to the ceremonially important east end. The hordes of tourists who flock to the Acropolis in the season may serve to give the impression of the crowds of worshippers. But nothing now recalls the smell of the sacrificial animals, and their slaughter which provided such a climax to the festival.

The architectural development of the Acropolis was virtually completed with the work of the fifth century. No one would have considered replacing these major monuments, and they were kept in repair. The Erechtheion was again severely damaged by fire in the first century BC, but the damage was made good under Roman auspices, great care being taken to copy and reproduce the forms of the original building. At the same time a small circular structure, in the Ionic order of the Erechtheion and dedicated to Rome and Augustus, was built in front of the Parthenon. So long as the cult of Athena continued in the Roman period her sanctuary, its buildings and monuments were maintained. Only in the Late Roman period under the new religion of Christianity did ruin set in. Even so the buildings were patched up and converted to those other purposes which at least guaranteed their partial survival to the present day.

The sanctuary of Hephaistos

In contrast, the sanctuary of Hephaistos above the agora has a much simpler history. It was not a major cult centre. It owes its architectural prominence partly to its direct relationship with the agora below and to the east, and partly to celebrate the contribution of the metal workers (who probably had a simple shrine here) to the defeat of the Persians. There may also be a specific connection with the occupation of Athens by the Persians whose armies seem to have camped out in this part of the city. The most interesting feature of this sanctuary, in addition to its temple, was the discovery of a series of pits cut into the rock along the south side of the temple, by each column. These contained flower pots for shrubs. A special water supply for them was also provided, probably in the third century BC, and other arrangements for plants were made on the opposite (north) side. This is the best evidence to survive for such treatment of sanctuaries, but the frequent references to them as sacred groves shows that this was a widespread and important characteristic of their appearance.

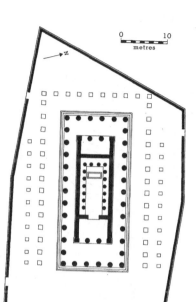

Fig. 34. Plan of the sanctuary of Hephaistos, Athens.

The sanctuary at Olympia

The sanctuary of Zeus at Olympia achieved major standing among all Greek cities – particularly those of the Peloponnese – very early on in their history. It is situated in fertile, well watered and wooded countryside on the western side of the Peloponnese in the valley of the river Alpheios, at its junction with a smaller tributary, the Kladeos. It is a rather gentle and attractive landscape, but it is some way from the more important Greek city states. A degree of religious continuity from the Bronze Age is probable, and in a sense it antedates the historical development of the Greek city states. Whether or not the Olympic Games go back as far as the traditional date for their foundation (in 776, or even earlier), Olympia was already an important sanctuary in the eighth century BC.

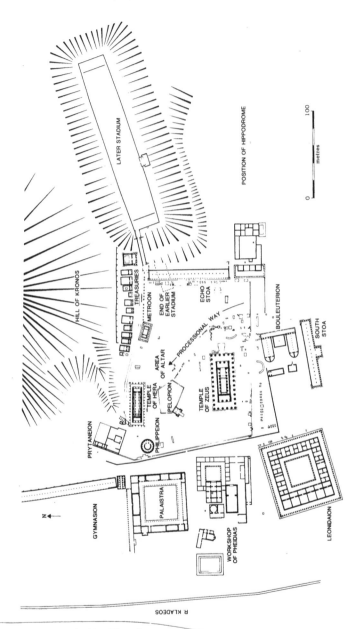

Fig. 35. Plan of Altis, Olympia.

The temple of Hera

The evidence for this, however, is not architectural. That it functioned then as a sanctuary is amply attested by the great quantities of offerings that have been found in the excavations there, particularly the simple figurines in bronze of geometric style going back to the tenth century. The oldest temple was that described by Pausanias as dedicated to Hera; it seems strange that Zeus' wife, rather than Zeus himself, should have been given the temple. It is no earlier than the first decade of the sixth century. Part of the cult image of Hera from this temple has survived – it was made of stone and wood – but this, also, cannot be earlier than the turn of the seventh and sixth centuries. If there was another image of Zeus, and a simple structure to house it, no evidence has survived for it. The sanctuary was known as the Altis, which means the grove: and its present park-like form with pine and Judas trees probably gives a fair impression of its ancient natural condition.

'The treasuries'

After the temple of Hera, the next important buildings were constructed along a terrace to the east between the temple and the stadium. These are the 'treasuries', temple-like buildings (built with two Doric columns for their porches) but not temples – since they did not contain cult-statues – dedicated to Zeus by individual Greek cities, usually as a thankoffering for a victory. They also function as treasuries in the literal sense, since they were the place for storing the valuable portable offerings made by the city which had dedicated them. Together, they demonstrate the importance of Olympia collectively to the Greek cities – international, in the sense that all Greeks respected it, though participation in the Games was firmly restricted to those who were recognized as Greeks.

From east to west in sequence the treasuries were dedicated by Sikyon, Syracuse, Epidauros, Byzantium, Sybaris. Of the next two, one is that of Cyrene, the other unknown, but it is not certain which is which (Pausanias mentions one – Cyrene, while the archaeologists have found two). Then follow Selinus, Metapontum, Megara, and Gela. This is a significant list, cities of the Dorian Peloponnese, or their overseas colonies, dominating (the importance of Olympia – on the west side of the Peloponnese – to the western colonies in Sicily is noticeable). Pausanias' dates for the erection of the various treasuries cause some problems. He tells us that that of Sikyon was dedicated by Myron, tyrant of the city, following his victory in the chariot race at the 33rd Olympic Games: that is, 648 BC. If so, it would be significantly older than the temple of Hera; but the form of the building shows that it was erected in the fifth century BC. That of Syracuse was a thankoffering for the victory at Himera, in 480 BC. By far the most splendid was the last in the sequence, that of Gela, which had a porch of six Doric columns in front of a cella whose roof, most unusually, seems to have had its ridge across its width rather than as a continuation of the porch roof. Immediately in front of the easternmost treasuries was the original running course of the stadium; later in the classical period this was moved further to the east, and enlarged. It was finally approached from the area in front of the treasuries by a vaulted tunnel, which, like those at Nemea and Epidauros, is Hellenistic in date.

Another early building is situated to the south of the sanctuary outside the (later) boundary wall, and therefore almost certainly not within the stricter limits of the sanctuary area. This consists of a pair of horseshoe-plan halls with a square room between them, and all united by an Ionic colonnade across the east front. Pausanias says that this is a council house: that is, the building for the committee (however it was chosen) who administered the Games. The form of the building goes back to the horseshoe-plan houses of Dark Age Greece; but the oldest part – the northernmost building – is only sixth-century in date, the southern belongs to the end of that century; the rest is a Hellenistic improvement.

The temple of Zeus

Undoubtedly the major architectural event of the fifth century was the construction of the great temple of Zeus (see Chapter 3 above). Its importance can be seen particularly in comparison with the other structures of the sanctuary which it dwarfs. Its position shows that it was not, however, the most important element in the sanctuary. In front of it passes the main route into the heart of the sanctuary, marked out more by the sequence of monuments which line it rather than any paving or formal treatment. This 'sacred way', or processional route, makes for the altar; the temple (and the statue it contains) merely look towards it, as the treasuries do at a greater distance on the northern side. Only the temple of Hera faces the area to which the sacred way leads, the place of sacrifice at the altar. The temple of Zeus is a commemorative monument, like the treasuries, but on a more substantial scale.

The prytaneion

One other building dates to the turn of the sixth and fifth centuries, the *prytaneion* to the north west of the temple of Hera, and set at an angle to it. Its original form cannot be elucidated – it underwent considerable modification in later times – but it appears to have functioned as a gathering place, probably with facilities for feasting. It consists of a series of rooms round a central open space or courtyard.

Other buildings at Olympia

Within the sanctuary, which must have been still recognizable as a grove, statues and other monuments lined the route to the altar (some of these were large, particularly the tall triangular pier which carried the statue of Winged Victory by Paionios, dedicated by the Messenians of Naupaktos). Buildings are arranged haphazardly – to no preconceived plan or alignment – to face the altar or the routes to the altar and other routes within the sacred area. To the east is the area set aside for the contests of the Games, the stadium. How far this was regarded as being inside or outside the sanctuary is difficult to determine. It is outside the later (Roman) boundary wall, but its function was evidently part of the sacred ritual. Probably we can see here (as in other sanctuaries, including Delphi) something of a two stage system: the innermost sacred area round the altar, the place of sacrifice, and including the temples; and an outer area, still sacred, but devoted more to the human aspects of ritual. The hippodrome, where the chariots raced, is part of the outer area. The races were already of considerable importance in the sixth century, but, like the contemporary stadium, the hippodrome received no architectural embellishment.

In subsequent years, a few more buildings are put up within the strictly sacred area: chiefly, in the fourth century, the small peripteral temple to the mother goddess, the Metroon, 10.62 x 20.67 m., with 6 x 11 Doric columns. It belongs to the early fourth century, and lies close to and in front of the terrace of the treasuries, to the east of the temple of Hera. To the west of the temple, later in the century, Alexander the Great built the small circular Ionic memorial to his father, the Philippeion, which once contained statues of Philip and his family. A long portico, the 'Echo Stoa' runs along the east side, facing towards the processional route and the temples, 98 m. in length. It belongs to the second half of the fourth century. Another stoa, to the south of the Bouleuterion (the 'south stoa') turns its back on the sanctuary and faces outwards, but still forms a defining element. To the west of the sanctuary is another cluster of lesser, ancillary buildings: the substantial hall which Pheidias used as his workshop when he created his gold and ivory statue of Zeus, and which was eventually converted into a church; a large courtyard building, given by one Leonidas of Naxos (not to be confused with the Spartan king who fell at Thermopylae) as a 'hotel' in which visitors to the sanctuary and its festival could be accommodated – its function shows that it was not part of the main sanctuary – and which was substantially rebuilt in the Roman period; further to the north, the wrestling ground, or *palaistra*, a Doric courtyard 41.42 x 41.52 m., with surrounding rooms (giving external dimensions of 66.35 x 66.75 m.). These rooms are not generally closed, but are approached from the peristyle through open colonnades rather than doors, and thus conform closely to Vitruvius' description of the Greek gymnasium. There are benches for sitting round the walls of several of the rooms. Vitruvius regards these as places where people could receive instruction, or engage in philosophical discussion. As a generalisation for gymnasia in Greek cities, this is likely enough, but the purpose to which these rooms were put at Olympia is less clear. To the north is the gymnasium proper, an enormous enclosed courtyard with flanking stoas. Its exact dimensions and extent are lost, washed away by the river Kladeos, but it was clearly large enough for athletic activities, such as running and throwing, for which the *palaistra* was too small. It is Hellenistic in date, like the *palaistra*.

Thus the boundaries were more clearly defined by buildings, as well as by the monuments related to them. The north boundary was delineated by the slopes of the 'Hill of Kronos' and the early buildings, temple and treasuries at its foot; the buildings of the other boundaries are later. A formal boundary wall was constructed only in the Roman period: it runs down the west side where it separates more completely the western ancillary buildings from the sacred area, but then returns to the east to form a southern boundary – in effect shutting out the south stoa and the Bouleuterion building. To the west of the Bouleuterion a magnificent gateway, in the form of a triumphal arch, belongs also to this Roman handling of the sanctuary boundaries. Other Roman buildings are outside the boundary, and consist of bath buildings and other ancillary structures. Unlike many Greek sanctuaries, Olympia flourished in the Roman period. Slow decay, the conversion of the empire and the closing of the pagan temples brought inevitable decline. The sanctuary was plundered by the barbarian Heruls in AD 267, and a fortification wall enclosing the temple of Zeus and the area to the south stoa was constructed against them. Final ruin came with the earthquake in the sixth century AD, after which the rivers contributed increasingly to the silting over and burial of much of the remains.

The sanctuary at Delphi

Like Olympia, Delphi was a major sanctuary whose importance was recognized by all Greek cities: indeed, from the indication of the monuments there it received major support from a wider range of them. Its special importance rested with its oracle whose significance is easily misunderstood as a mere foreteller of the future. It advised on the proper course of action. It also gave advice on religious procedures: there was no central organization, in any form, for Greek religion. It was only through prestige and experience, and so reputation, that the Delphic oracle could tell what forms of ritual were fitting, rather than through any authority in the dogmatic sense. It is situated on a narrow shelf of land on the southern side of Mt. Parnassos, high above the plain of Amphissa – carpeted today with olive trees. In Classical times, as now, there was a small town which made its living more from the visitors than agriculture or trade.

The sanctuary itself was administered by a committee, the Amphictyonic Council, on which were represented those neighbouring (the meaning of the name) and more important Greek states. The oracle itself was a priestess, the Pythia, who seems to have ranted and raved. What she meant had to be interpreted for her; and it was the priests who presented the interpretation, who gave the real meaning to her replies, and whose experience, in all cases, controlled the answers. As so frequently, the locality seems to have had religious significance dating back at least to the Late Bronze Age: the legends attached to the sanctuary imply some discontinuity – of the 'take over' of the sanctuary by Apollo as an intruder – a legend which may reflect the upheaval of the Dark Age. The significance of the place depends subjectively on the general atmosphere; more objectively on its

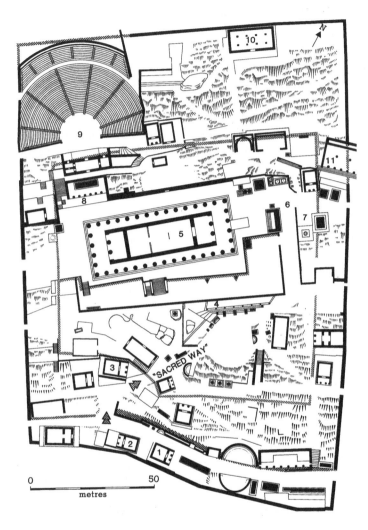

Fig. 36. Plan of the sanctuary of Apollo, Delphi.

1 *Treasury of Sikyon*
2 *Treasury of Siphnos*
3 *Treasury of the Athenians*
4 *Stoa of the Athenians*
5 *Temple of Apollo*
6 *Altar of Apollo (of the Chians)*

7 *The Monument of Plataea*
8 *The Lion Hunt of Alexander*
 (Krateros' Monument)
9 *The Theatre*
10 *The Lesche of the Knidians*
11 *The Stoa of Attalos*

superb, abundant and pure water supplies, in particular the fountain of Castalia. Besides the main sanctuary of Apollo, west of Castalia, there is, to the east, a second sanctuary of Athena. The sanctuary is placed on a fairly steep slope. Buildings normally depend on substantial terracing to give them a level platform, and this breaks up the sanctuary much more than the relatively level areas of the Athenian Acropolis, or the totally flat sanctuary at Olympia. There is no extensive flat area where the crowds of worshippers could gather, even round the altar. The sacred area is marked off by a precinct wall, defining it precisely and dating back to the sixth century BC (though with a later extension). The entrance is at the south eastern corner, the route for approaching after the purification rituals in the spring of Castalia. There is no formal gateway, merely an opening into the extensive area of the sanctuary. The route passed below what was previously the southern edge of the sanctuary, then zig-zagged back and up towards the eastern end of the temple and the altar. As at Olympia, this 'sacred way' was the obvious approach route for processions within the sanctuary; only in Roman times was it paved as a formal road.

The temple of Apollo

Fig. 37. View of the sanctuary of Apollo, Delphi.

In Classical times the temple stood on a very substantial platform of which it occupied the greater part. This was supported by a splendid terrace wall built from blocks fitted in a 'crazy paving' technique, with curving lines to many of the joints – a technique briefly in favour late in the sixth century. There were earlier temples, and presumably earlier platforms, but it is the sixth-century platform which still dominates the sanctuary. The temple measures 21.68 x 58.18 m. and had 6 x 15 Doric columns. There is a ramp approach onto the platform at the eastern end. Compared with other temples it is long in relation to its width. This is not simply an archaic feature: the greater length of the cella was necessary to house the inner sanctum, which was fenced off from the main part of the cella, where the Pythia was consulted. This temple stood until the mid-fourth century, when it was ruined as a result of a fall of rock from the cliffs above. It was rebuilt – the funds being raised by a general collection – to the same plan exactly, since religious usage had clearly determined this. Its date of destruction is uncertain. Delphi had periods of decline, and Plutarch wrote about the waning of oracles; but, judging from the monuments, it still flourished as a sanctuary. There was a deliberate rehabilitation early in the third century AD; but when it was visited by the emperor Julian in the 360s – the last recorded consultation of the oracle – the reply 'say to the king the well-wrought hall has fallen to the ground...' suggests that it was in ruins.

The Siphnian and Athenian treasuries

Like Olympia, the sanctuary at Delphi is also full of dedications from individual Greek cities, commemorating victories and other benefaction for which they felt the need to thank Apollo. They include treasuries, similar to those at Olympia. They were built by a wider range of Greek cities than at Olympia, and include Ionic examples, such as the splendid treasury of the Siphnians, built about 524 to give thanks not for a victory but rather the discovery of a rich vein of silver on the island. This stands on a high platform built from local limestone, and originally outside the precinct (though it was included, like its neighbours, in the subsequent extension). The superstructure is entirely marble – Siphnian, Naxian and Parian, making this probably the earliest fully marble building in mainland Greece. It was lavishly decorated with sculpture, and in place of conventional columns two statues of maidens (caryatids) formed the porch. Another, slightly later Dorian treasury, higher up the sacred

Fig. 38. Treasury of the Athenians, Delphi.

way, is that of the Athenians, probably built as a thankoffering for Marathon; though it was completely ruined much of the super-structure remained, and it has been largely reconstructed.

The altar of Apollo and other dedications

The altar of Apollo was a gift from the Ionian island of Chios. Adjacent to it on the platform of the temple are several other dedications which indicate the support Apollo received from the whole of the Greek world and even beyond: a large monument set up by the Syracusans, Hellenistic monuments to the rulers of Bithynia, private dedication for prominent inhabitants of Aetolia (the region of Greece which dominated Delphi for much of the Hellenistic period) and so forth. Opposite the altar on the other side of the approach route was the bronze tripod supported on a snake base, set up for the victory at Plataea. The enclosed area continued above the temple, with more statue monuments. At the very top was the club-house (*Lesche*) of the Cnidians, an enclosed fifth-century building which probably functioned as a banqueting hall. Later structures in this northern part include a dedication by the Macedonian Krateros, depicting Alexander the Great's lion hunt; and above this, the theatre, relatively small and apparently something of an afterthought. This is the only place within the boundary of the sanctuary where a large number of worshippers could gather, though it is clearly not intended as a viewing place for the altar.

Stoas and the stadium

Other structures are outside the precinct wall (though one, a Hellenistic stoa given by King Attalus of Pergamon, actually breaches the wall). There is another long stoa on the western side; but the most important structure is the stadium for the Pythian games, on another terrace to the south-west of the sanctuary, placed remotely because of the difficulty of finding a sufficient level ground for both running course and spectators. Presumably the games were always held here (as early as the sixth century BC), though the provision of formal stone seating is later.

The sanctuary of Athena

The other sanctuary, of Athena, is also situated on a different terrace, below the main sanctuary and further to the east. Here are the remains of a succession of temples, from the seventh century to the fourth, the earlier still showing the damage from falling rock which necessitated their replacement on a different position. Here, too, there is another of the rare circular monuments, the Tholos, of unknown purpose and origin. It is built with slender Doric columns which suggest a fourth-century date; though this may result rather from the particular needs of proportion in circular structures using columns which were developed from rectangular buildings (there are the remains of another, sixth-century Tholos in the sanctuary of Apollo, moved from an unknown position to be incorporated in the substructure of the Treasury of Sikyon, next door to that of Siphnos). Athena also has a number of treasuries, including one given by the city of Massalia (Marseilles) with strange uncanonical columns, best described as palm tree in style; also found, much later, in the architecture of Pergamon, and suggesting an origin in that part of the world (Massalia was colonized by Phocaea, from this region). Another building, later obliterated by the fourth-century temple, contained an antechamber and two eleven-couch dining rooms. Finally, immediately to the west of the Athena sanctuary but not functionally attached to it was an area for athletic exercise, or gymnasium, including a circular plunge bath. This area seems to be largely Hellenistic in date.

Fig. 39. The Tholos, Delphi.

These major sanctuaries developed on an abnormal scale, with particularly magnificent buildings, for various but essentially extraordinary reasons. Other sanctuaries may rival them in importance (Delos) or the magnificence of their temples (the East Greek sanctuaries of Hera, Samos; Artemis, Ephesos; or Apollo, Didyma). But the majority were much humbler in scale, and in the dedications made to them. Yet they had the same essential function and responded to the same religious needs, but for a smaller, or more impoverished circle of worshippers. Each had its own independent administration, its own finances, and was built in a way which suited both. They are all, equally, an essential part of Classical Greek life.

Chapter 6
Buildings in their Context – Cities

In the same way, the cities of Classical Greece differ widely in size, wealth and architectural magnificence. Their buildings do not stand in isolation but are related to each other, visually and functionally. The dense packed houses cannot be appreciated without understanding their relationship to the public buildings (including, of course, the temples) and the varying arrangements of them. Similarly, the open spaces do not make full architectural sense except in the context of the buildings that surround them. It is misleading to treat buildings as if they existed in total isolation.

The result of natural development

Greek cities are either the result of natural, gradual development, or are deliberately created by planning. The first category consists of places whose origins are unknown, and probably remote from the Classical period; the second includes colonies, and cities created on new sites, or moved to them from old sites for strategic or political purposes. The first often go back to the Bronze Age – at least the Late Bronze Age, the Mycenaean world, but in some cases possibly as far back as the early Bronze Age, or even the Neolithic period. This does not necessarily mean that they were inhabited continuously from these remote times. Even the question of continuity from the final years of the Late Bronze Age through the succeeding Dark Age into the Classical period is one which is endlessly debated by archaeologists, and there may well be changes of population from age to age. For the architecture, more important are the reasons why a particular site should attract occupation. These include the necessary economic support for the community (that is, agricultural land above everything else), security and defence, and availability of water supplies. A site such as the Acropolis of Athens is a natural focus for settlement, and habitation developed here of its own accord, without any element of formal planning. The Athenians, in fact, believed that their ancestors had always inhabited the same place; and here the possibility of real continuity from the Late Bronze Age to the Classical city is very persuasive. Athens serves as a good, first ranking example of our first category of city.

Classical Athens

The plan of Classical Athens is determined first by the Acropolis. Initially a citadel, with massive prehistoric fortifications, it continued as a place of refuge in the Dark Age; though as with the Bronze Age citadels, the ordinary population seems to have lived outside the walls on the lower slopes of the Acropolis hill and the surrounding areas. The Acropolis itself was relatively inaccessible, approached easily only from its western end, and routes of communication had to go round rather than across it. These routes depend on the local geography and always take the line of least difficulty: they wind their way up the hillsides and valleys, easing the slope as much as possible. They avoid natural obstacles. They connect different places on behalf

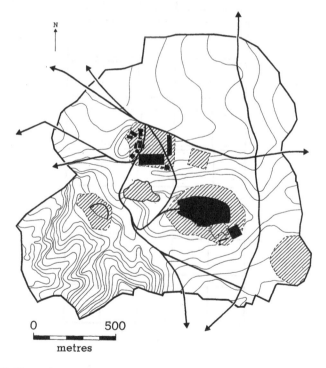

Fig. 40. General arrangement plan of Athens.

of people who need to move from one to the other. They provide short cuts. Thus the lines of the streets, and the siting of different structures in the street plan, depend on chance and natural development. A totally irregular plan, and a largely irregular choice of locality for the different essential elements within the plan, is the hallmark of a traditional, naturally developing city.

The planned city

The second category of city arises in totally different circumstances, and is the result of a deliberate decision by an individual or group of

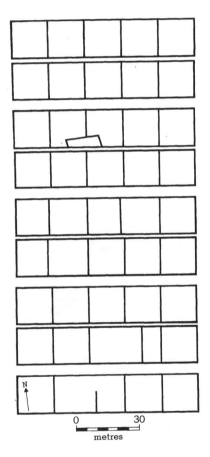

Fig. 41. House plots, Olynthus.

individuals acting together, to place a new community at a pre-determined site. The sensible town planner looks for the same advantages – economy, defence, water supply – since without them his new community is unlikely to flourish, but he imposes his plan on the site. Within the plan he has to make allocations: not only for temples and the other public buildings, for the public open spaces and amenities, but also to individual families where they can build their houses. He has to do this in a way which is accepted as fair and is simple to administer. So he draws up a regular street plan, with straight roads crossing at right angles and forming a grid. This makes possible a series of standard-sized, perfectly rectangular building plots which can be fairly and properly allocated. This is the hallmark of the planned city. Although variations may be introduced subsequently, the original grid, imposed often with little regard for the lie of the land or the problems this causes, demonstrates its origins.

Priene

The classic example of such a city is Priene. Situated on the northern side of the estuary of the river Maeander in Ionia (opposite Miletus), its origins go back to around 1000 BC. However, it was moved to a new site (or perhaps the inhabitants collected from a number of sites), probably about 350 BC, for reasons which are quite unknown. The new site was a shelf of land above the flood plain of the river, reasonably level but sloping more steeply at its extremities. It had the advantage of good agricultural land in the vicinity (though not a large area: Priene was only a small place) but it was not a first rate defensive position (this was achieved by surrounding the entire site with up-to-date fortifications, and by attaching to the city a separate fortified Acropolis on the top of the hill behind it). Nor did it have good water supplies on the site itself (water was provided by an aqueduct from a spring in the hills behind, and then piped to the various parts of the city). The streets are arranged to form a grid whose lines run E-W and N-S. The east to west lines are reasonably level, rising gradually from the west to the centre. One street is marked out as a principal street and runs from a gate in the city wall to the agora at the centre of the plan; it was obviously used by wheeled traffic. Many of the N-S streets are much steeper, and in their steepest sections are flights of steps rather than roads. Not all the area available within the fortification was built over.

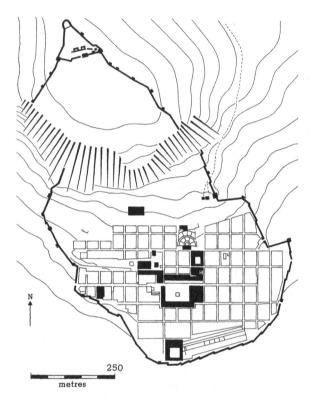

Fig. 42. Plan of Priene.

The city defined by its boundaries

In their developed form all Greek cities have a defined boundary, not necessarily coincidental with the built up area, and not necessarily fixed. Burial of the dead within the boundary is prohibited, and graves are found lining the roads which radiate from the town beyond its boundaries. Houses may be built beyond the city limits as need arises but, apart from city suburbs, people living outside the town usually prefer to cluster in villages rather than live in isolated rural houses. The boundary often coincides with a line of fortification. In planned cities a line of defences is normally part of the original design, as at Priene. Unplanned cities may develop, as does Athens, by clustering round a citadel, but an outer defence at the boundary is usually constructed. This, however, is not inevitable, and Classical Sparta, a grouping of four villages, remained unfortified. Athens seems to have acquired walls either in the late sixth century before the Persian wars, or after the recovery of the captured city from Xerxes – the walls built by Themistocles. When walls existed they were a very important part of the city architecturally: they were the part seen by people approaching from outside, and gave a clear definition to the structure of the city. They were designed to be imposing and even if (as at Classical Athens) the superstructure was only mudbrick, they were plastered and whitewashed – partly to protect, but also to improve their appearance. Their gates gave a sense of movement from the world outside to the world within, analogous to the passage from the secular to the religious world of the sanctuary.

The chief sanctuary

Within its walls the city may be dominated by its chief sanctuary, particularly if, as at Athens, this is sited on a demilitarised former citadel; but this is not inevitable. At Priene, the chief temple is placed on a conveniently high area within the city plan, but the citadel is elsewhere. At some cities the chief sanctuary is not within the city limits at all, but outside. Thus a major temple may be the most important building within the city, but this is by no means essential or invariable.

The agora

More important to the city plan and the context of its buildings is the agora. It is generally located towards the centre: this is certainly true at Priene, where it is the agora, not the temple, which is at the centre of the grid plan. Centrality at Athens is made impossible by the existence of the Acropolis, but the agora is reasonably centred within the important area to the north of it. Cities immediately adjacent to the sea, such as Piraeus, often have their agoras by the harbour, since that also serves as a focal element; and it is useful to have the two together. The agora is invariably defined with the original setting out of planned cities, but this is not always so in the unplanned. At Athens it appears at a relatively late stage in the city's organic growth, where the original focus may have been rather the Acropolis. When the Athenian agora developed (not until the sixth century BC), it was in the most convenient flat area at the northern foot of the Acropolis.

Fig. 43. The agora at Athens, viewed from the Acropolis.

This area seems at the time not to have been covered by the extending spread of houses because it was waterlogged from the springs on the side of the Acropolis. It therefore had to be drained and prepared before it could function. This happened at about the same time that the city reached its full limits, when the fortification wall was built.

Waterworks

Thus the general form of a Greek city, to which its buildings are essentially subordinated, depends on three elements: the boundary, whether or not delineated by a visually impressive wall and gates; the street plan, whether planned or unplanned; and the agora at its focus. The distribution of buildings within this plan depends on function. Some are placed as a result of geographical factors. Fountain houses, in the form of porticoes which shade spouts through which water can be taken, usually depend on the position of the springs which feed them. In Athens Klepsydra is situated high on the north-west slopes of the Acropolis; Enneakrounos is lower down, in the area of the agora; while at Corinth, Peirene is by an abundant source. Alternatively, as at Priene, water may be brought into the city in conduits and piped to appropriate draw points. The construction of waterworks is an important branch of Greek architecture, in which the use of hydraulic cement is developed in order to line the supply conduits and storage basins.

Administration buildings

Administrative buildings tend to be collected around or in the vicinity of the agora. The agora at Athens had on its western edge the Stoa of the King, where the *Basileus archon* conducted trials in those religious matters which remained his administrative responsibility even in the fifth-century democracy. There were the noticeboards on which copies of new decrees were posted, and the archive where they were stored. There was the meeting house of the democratic Council, the *Boule*. There was the circular *tholos*, where the standing Committee of the Council, the *prytaneis*, who were on duty for a month at a time, feasted. Beyond this, by a street leading away from the agora, was a building which probably functioned as a prison. On the south side, in addition to Enneakrounos, was the building for the citizen jury court (the *Heliaia*), and the mint. Round the agora were shrines, small temples (to Zeus, to Apollo Patroos, to Hekate), and stoas which provided shelter and dining accommodation for the citizens. All these were placed irregularly but, being on the perimeter of the agora, define its extent.

At Priene, on the other hand, the agora has become more formalised. It consists of two 'blocks' of the city grid plan. Whereas in Athens the agora was a nodal part for city streets which ran to it, through it, and out again, at Priene only the main east-west street passed through (or, to be precise, along one side of) the agora; other, lesser streets were either interrupted, or diverted to pass outside it. Its area was regular and rectangular, not an odd-shaped plan which happened to be available, as at Athens, and it takes the form of a courtyard edged with stoas. One stoa lined the northern boundary, with the east-west street running in front of it; the three other sides were defined by a continuous colonnade. Within the agora there were monuments, but no buildings. Rooms at the back of the original north stoa (it was later rebuilt and extended further to the east, but still retained its rooms) seem to have had an administrative function, and public records were inscribed on its walls. There was a separate building for a Council (or, given that Priene is a small place, a restricted citizen assembly) to one side, and, further away, another building may have been an official dining room. Priene's agora is more simple in plan, and the location of different functions not precisely the same as at Athens; but in the arrangement of the city, it is directly comparable. The agora at Athens was 'modernized' in the second century BC by a series of new, large stoas placed at right angles, to resemble more closely the regular form the agora had taken in the planned cities.

Theatres

Other public buildings are found in different parts of the city plan. The theatre, whether as a separate building or element in a sanctuary of Dionysus, requires if possible a suitable hillside for its auditorium. Only in places which are built, most exceptionally, on totally flat ground, such as Mantinea, can the theatre (which now requires artificial substructures for support) be built anywhere in the plan, and so be deliberately attached to the agora (theatres often doubled as political meeting places). At Athens the theatre of Dionysus was attached to the sanctuary of that god, on the south slopes of the Acropolis which supported the auditorium. At Priene the theatre is placed where the shelf on which the city is built begins to rise more steeply as the Acropolis hill, to give the right elevation for the auditorium; but here it is at the very edge of the developed area. There is, as at Athens, some terracing support; but a noticeable difference is that the seats are truncated in order to contain the auditorium within the rectangular ground space demarcated, even on the hill slope, by the city plan (a similarly truncated theatre, like Priene of Hellenistic date, also occurs in the non-planned town of Thera).

Gymnasia

The gymnasia of Athens and Priene differ considerably, but this is not because of the nature of the street plan. The gymnasia at Athens are little known, and little preserved. There are remains of the Academy, which suggest part of it was given a courtyard, possibly colonnaded, but of the Lyceum and Kynosarges even less is known. They are all situated outside the city boundary, open spaces devoted to exercise and the practice of the hoplite military skills which were the essence of the citizen army of the Classical city. The development of the Academy by Plato, and the Lyceum by Aristotle, as philosophical schools, is an additional function. Priene had its own soldiers, but serious warfare in the Hellenistic age was left to the armies of the kings, and the citizens of Priene in the third and second centuries did not undergo the same military training as the youth of Athens in the fifth. At Priene the gymnasia are more obviously schools. They are therefore to be found within the city area: one near the centre, the other, with the adjacent stadium, added at a convenient place against the walls at the lowest point of the city site.

Houses

Most of the city area was devoted to houses. A distinction needs to be made between the population who lived within the city walls, and the much larger population of the city state, the majority of whom normally lived outside the walls and mostly in villages. Even a large city, such as Athens, did not house the majority of the citizens (Hellenistic Alexandria may have been an exception to this general rule, a city whose citizens lived mostly within the city limits; but Alexandria was not a normal Greek city). At Priene there was a distinction between citizens and other inhabitants of the state who did not possess citizenship: of those who were citizens, perhaps a greater proportion had houses in the city than at Athens, but the majority of the population surely lived outside. Possession of a house inside the city of Priene may well have been a privilege of citizenship; at Athens, on the other hand, it was due more to geographical chance, and did not imply any particular status. In both Athens and Priene and, indeed, all Greek cities, the public buildings had to cater for more than those living within the walls: they had to cater for the population of the entire state. They were therefore larger than the city population warranted.

Thus in most Greek cities public buildings and public open spaces occupied a greater proportion of the city area than is the case with modern towns. Houses were relatively densely packed into the remaining space, whether they were of the varying shapes and sizes found in unplanned cities, or of the more regular, rectilinear shapes in planned cities such as Priene. In some cities – Olynthus and Piraeus were examples – large areas of houses seem to have been built on predetermined plots to precisely standard dimensions.

Houses were built with their outer walls directly lining the street. Within the street block, whether irregular or regular in shape, there would be several houses in direct contact with each other and sharing party walls – the latter an obvious cause of neighbourly disputes (we have the text of building regulations at Pergamon, which are very strict about party walls). Since they were lit largely from the interior courtyard, any windows in exterior walls were small, high in the wall and inaccessible. The streets, whether the winding alleys of unplanned cities or the straight lines of the grid plan cities, were thus lined with plain walls, usually of mudbrick, and punctuated principally by the doors. The effect can best be experienced at Hellenistic Delos where the houses were built of stone, and therefore reasonably well preserved. To walk these streets is essentially the same experience as walking the streets of the modern town – on neighbouring Mykonos. In the Classical city lines of houses, undifferentiated and visually uninteresting, dominate the enclosed area. But they are punctuated by the sudden emergence into an open space, a space always surrounded by buildings – increasingly of architectural splendour. It is in such a context that we must visualize the more important of Classical buildings in order to appreciate both their architecture and their contribution to the life of the people who inhabited and used them.

Fig. 44. Houses on Delos.

Suggestions for Further Study

A short book such as this one can include only a very small selection of examples from Greek architecture. It is useful to compare them with others.

To what extent do the arrangements in the major sanctuaries such as Olympia and Delphi correspond to those in sanctuaries of less importance (for example, Artemis at Brauron)? What categories of building are found in the major international sanctuaries and not in the lesser, local examples? Why should this be so?

It is also useful to compare individual examples of the different categories of building: to the uninitiated all Greek temples look alike, but this is not so. Compare the major temples – Zeus, Olympia, or the Parthenon with less important sanctuaries, such as the temple of Hera at Perachora. Some temples have very distinctive arrangements: look up the temple of Apollo at Didyma, and see how it modified standard temple form. What are the reasons for this?

Regional variations in Greek architecture are not inconsiderable. The difference between mainland (Doric) and East Greece (Ionic) is obvious, but what other variations are there? Try to isolate the special characteristics of distinctive regional form, such as that found in Sicily, or even more limited areas, such as Boeotia.

What about the architecture of classical Sparta? Thucydides commented: 'Suppose that the city of Sparta became deserted, so that only foundations of temples and other buildings remained, I think that future generations would find it very difficult to believe that the place was really as powerful as it was said to be.' Why is this so amply borne out by the archaeological evidence? To answer this it is necessary to consider the economic implications of building, the availability of funds and labour, to see how architecture responds to the political and economic circumstances of the time.

Suggestions for Further Reading

Lawrence, A.W., *Greek Architecture* (Harmondsworth, Penguin, 4th ed. 1983). A copiously illustrated book, which discusses a good cross section of buildings from the earliest architecture of the Aegean Bronze Age to the Hellenistic period. Full up-to-date bibliography.

Dinsmoor, W.B., *The Architecture of Ancient Greece* (London, Batsford, 1950). An encyclopaedic description of Classical Greek architecture, and an essential reference book. It contains a very full glossary of architectural technical terms.

Coulton, J.J., *Greek Architects at Work* (London, Elek, 1977). A full account of the way in which Greek buildings were designed, and the methods employed in their construction.

Wycherley, R.E., *How the Greeks Built Cities* (London, Macmillan, 1949). A basic and readable book describing the architectural arrangements of Greek cities, and the various types of public buildings to be found in them.

Tomlinson, R.A., *Greek Sanctuaries* (London, Elek, 1976). An account of the arrangements in sanctuaries of different types, emphasizing their religious functions, and giving a more detailed account of a cross section taken from different regions and examples of varying rank.

Travlos, J., *Pictorial Dictionary of Ancient Athens* (London, Thames and Hudson, 1977). Lavishly illustrated with first-rate photographs and many original plans and other drawings by the author, with brief explanatory text and bibliography.

Boersma, J.S., *Athenian Building Policy from 561/0 to 405/4 BC* (Groningen, Wolters Noordhoff Publishing, 1970). A detailed analysis of the political circumstances and background to the creation of Athenian Classical architecture, with a good catalogue (with diagrammatic plans) of all buildings known from this period.

Fletcher, Sir Bannister, *A History of Architecture on the Comparative Method* (London, Butterworth, 19th ed. 1987). Part 1 of this gives an up-to-date synopsis of Greek and Hellenistic architecture, along with other chapters on other ancient Mediterranean architecture which put the Greek in its wider historical context. It also contains a colour photograph of the Tomb of Philip of Macedon which illustrates the use of painted decoration in Greek architecture.

Two volumes in the series 'The Making of the Past' (London, Elsevier-Phaidon, 1976), *The Emergence of Greece* by Alan Johnston and *The Greek World* by Roger Ling put Greek Architecture in the general context of the art and historical development of the archaic and Classical periods.

Other books, and specialised studies, including important books in foreign languages:

Martin, R., *Manuel d'architecture grecque* (Paris, Picard, 1965).

Broneer, O., *Isthmia, The Temple of Poseidon* (Princeton, Princeton University Press, 1971).

Hodge, A.T., *The Woodwork of Greek Roofs* (Cambridge, Cambridge University Press, 1960).

Mallwitz, A., *Olympia und seine Bauten* (Munich, Prestel Verlag, 1972).

Fouilles de Delphes: volumes in Part II, *Architecture* (De Boccard, 1915 onwards).

Burford, A., *The Temple Builders of Epidauros* (Liverpool, Liverpool University Press, 1969).

Doxiades, C., *Architectural Space in Ancient Greece* (Cambridge Mass., Harvard University Press, 1972).

Penrose, F.C., *An Investigation of the Principles of Athenian Architecture* (London, Dilettanti Society, 1888).

Ecole Française d'Athènes, *Exploration Archéologique de Délos* (De Boccard).

Wiegand, T. and Shrader, H., *Priene* (Berlin, Reimer, 1904).

Coulton, J.J., *The Architectural Development of the Greek Stoa* (Oxford, Oxford University Press, 1976).

Martin, R., *L'urbanisme dans la Grèce Antique* (Paris, Picard, 1951).

Glossary of Technical Terms

The different parts of buildings are often most economically described by an established technical term. This list includes those used in this book, to describe essential parts of Greek buildings. Fuller lists will be found in the comprehensive handbooks, such as Dinsmoor's *Architecture of Ancient Greece*. Many of these terms are in fact the appropriate Ancient Greek word, or the Latin equivalent.

abacus The square bearing-section at the top of a capital.

acroterion Decoration (often carved figures) standing on and decorating the three angles of a pediment.

agora An open space within (or, at times, outside) Greek cities, as a gathering place for the inhabitants, for religious as well as political meetings and commerce.

andron Dining room (for male guests) in Greek houses and public buildings.

anta The decorative termination of the side walls of temples or similiar buildings.

antefix A decorative element, either of terracotta or carved in stone, masking the ends of the ridge tiles which cover the joints between adjacent flat (pan) tiles in the roofs of Greek buildings which do not have simas (gutters).

architrave The series of beams supported by the columns.

bouleuterion The building in which the city council (*boule*) met.

capital The bearing element at the top of a column.

cella The main 'room' of temple, containing the statue of the god or gods to whom the building was dedicated.

Corinthian The third order of Greek architecture, similar to Ionic, but using elaborate capitals with four volutes (meeting at angles) over double rows of carved leaves, derived from those of the acanthus plant.

cornice A series of continuous blocks projecting forwards above the frieze or at the top of a wall and intended to throw the rainwater falling on the roof behind them clear of the colonnade or wall beneath.

dentils Series of small block-like projections in the frieze of Ionic temples, resembling small beam ends.

dipteral Temples surrounded by double rows of columns.

Doric The order (q.v.) used for temples in mainland Greece and the West.

echinus The spreading section, circular in plan, of a Doric capital, where it is plain, or of an Ionic capital, where it is given carved decoration.

entablature The entire superstructure (architrave, frieze, cornice) supported by the columns.

entasis The slightly curved profile given to column shafts in major buildings.

fascia A flat band: particularly the three fasciae of Ionic architraves.

flute (or fluting) The vertical channels which form a decorative treatment to the shafts of columns.

frieze A second series of blocks coming directly on top of the architrave (q.v.).

geison A Greek word for cornice (q.v.).

guttae Projecting flat cylindrical discs, probably representing wooden pegs originally, under the Doric regulae and mutules (q.v.).

hekatompedon A 'hundred footer'. That is, a substantial temple, at least 100 feet in length.

hippodrome A race course for chariots.

Ionic The order (q.v.) used originally for temples in the East Greek area and the Aegean.

megaron In the Homeric poems, the principal room of a palace. In architecture a rectangular room whose side walls are extended at one end to form a porch.

metopes Flat slabs, alternating with triglyphs (q.v.) to make up the Doric frieze. They may be left plain, or decorated with painting or sculpture in relief.

mutules Flat blocks (decorated with guttae, q.v.) under the Doric cornice (q.v.).

odeion Music hall.

orchestra The circular dancing floor for the chorus in Greek theatre buildings.

order The type of columns used in Greek buildings, together with their entablature (q.v.).

parodos walls The side walls supporting the ends of the seating in

Greek theatres.

pediment The gable end of a roof.

peripteral A temple with external colonnades all round. That is, at the sides as well as the ends.

propylon, propylaia The gateway building in Greek sanctuaries.

prytanieion Meeting place of the Prytaneis, or subcommittee of the Council.

pseudodipteral Temples on whose bases there is space for two surrounding rows of columns (i.e. dipteral) but on which only the outer row was actually erected.

raking cornice The cornice (q.v.) on the pediments (gable ends).

regulae Projections carved in the same block of stone placed at intervals under the Doric tainia.

sima A gutter, either carved in stone or moulded in terracotta at the bottom of the roof.

stoa A portico.

stylobate The top step of a temple on which the columns stand.

tainia A projecting band running along the top of the Doric architrave (q.v.). This would have been given painted decoration, but this is well preserved only on the facades of the buried Macedonian tombs.

terracotta Baked clay.

triglyph ('triple grooved') Rectangular blocks, decorated with V-sectioned vertical grooves which separate (and often hold in place) the metopes (q.v.) of the Doric frieze.

vernacular Built in the local style of ordinary houses.

volute The spirals decorating Ionic capitals.

CPSIA information can be obtained at www.ICGtesting.com
Printed in the USA
LVOW01s1708300714

396753LV00021B/1013/P